LIVERPOOL'S
OWN

LIVERPOOL'S OWN

CHRISTINE DAWE

THE HISTORY PRESS

The History Press
The Mill · Brimscombe Port · Stroud
Gloucestershire · GL5 2QG

First published 2008

British Library Cataloguing in Publication Data
A catalogue record for this book is available from
the British Library.

ISBN 978-07509-5049-7

Typeset in 10.5/13.5 Sabon.
Typesetting and origination by
The History Press.
Printed and bound in England.

*This book is dedicated to
the two most wonderful men in my life*

Picture Credits

The author is indebted to the following people and organisations for permission to
use photographs in this book.

Alan Bleasdale
Jean Boht
Tony Booth
Liverpool Central Library
Liverpool Football Club
Carl Davis
Liverpool Daily Post & Echo
Mersey Television
Cain's Brewery
Joan Finn
City magazine
Anthony George
Mersey Kidney Research
Geoffrey Hughes
Carla Lane

Angus Tilston
Sharon Maughan
Peter Ware
Nugent Care Society
Trevor Owens
Derek Holden
Anne Robinson
Walker Art Gallery
Alison Steadman
Clive Swift
David Swift
Liverpool Medical Institution
Ronald McDonald House
Sophie Baker

Contents

Foreword
by Peter Sissons

Every address in Liverpool and Merseyside should have a copy of *Liverpool's Own*. Whether, like me, you were born here, or have simply adopted this great city as your home, it is a compelling read. Of course, no one ever adopted Liverpool – the city does the adopting.

Within the pages of *Liverpool's Own* is a reminder of the city's uncanny ability not just to produce so much talent, but to turn so many extraordinary people into honorary Liverpudlians, inspiring them with a lifelong loyalty and affection for this special place, and drawing out of them some of their finest work. Wherever you come from, be it high or low, if you have something to give to Liverpool, then Liverpool will never forget you.

All Liverpudlians know that their city and its surroundings are special. They feel it in their bones. To outsiders, some can seem aggressive and arrogant about it. Others manifest their pride with a hurt defensiveness that unkind and ignorant outsiders characterise as mawkishness. To them it seems that the metropolitan media miss no chance to get on their backs. The critics forget that this was once one of the greatest port cities in the world – and that there was more than a geographical reason for it.

Now Liverpool again is resurgent, reminding the world of its cultural and sporting wealth, and its artistic, scientific, philanthropic and charitable heritage. So what better time to celebrate the great roll-call of those who made the city what it is?

But hold on! Although we know Liverpool is a special place, how many of us can name the people who made it special – and who gave the city, and in many cases the world, so much? We'll be able to name some, but within these pages is a glorious list of Liverpool and Merseyside's sons and daughters second to none. Their collective impact on the city, the nation, and in many cases the world is inestimable. Famous names like Gladstone, Shankly, Dodd, Leverhulme, McCartney, Rattle and scores more besides. Scientists, doctors, artists, entertainers, the high-born and the humble. And running through it all a thread of philanthropy and concern for their fellow men and women which is woven deep into Liverpool's heritage. These are people who not only cared about Liverpool, they cared about humanity.

To understand Liverpool, to understand its present and its future, and the hold that it has on those who count themselves fortunate to be part of it, just get to know *Liverpool's Own*. And, if you seek a monument to these extraordinary people, go to Merseyside and just look around you.

Introduction
Hims (and Hers) Ancient & Modern

There are many worthy tomes concerning Liverpool, the growth of the city and its beautiful architecture. There are histories of Merseyside's dark days in the nineteenth century and there are biographies galore of local politicians, sports stars, pop groups and famous show business figures.

This book is a pot-pourri of all these – a celebration and a commemoration of Merseyside's most colourful, charismatic or eccentric personalities, both past and present. Their achievements are possibly already well known, but I have attempted to present 'the stories behind the stories', so that the reader may make a more personal acquaintance with those who might be household names but whose backgrounds may not be so familiar.

My research has brought to my attention the determination and dedication shown by so many Scousers in their journeys towards success. Some of the most honoured and celebrated people came from humble or tragic beginnings. Others, with the good fortune of parental support and encouragement, have used their abilities to enrich the lives of others, either by philanthropic generosity, by striving for better working conditions or by giving the gift of laughter or sporting pride.

I was surprised and delighted to learn of the great diversity of charitable endeavour on Merseyside. Many organisations are of national origin, while others have actually been founded by the initiative of Liverpool's own, right here on our doorstep.

It has been a great pleasure to discover so much good news and to meet so many praiseworthy notables. I hope readers will enjoy being introduced to their Merseyside ancestors and to their present-day friends and neighbours as much as I have enjoyed the research.

Christine Dawe
Liverpool, 2008

About the Author

Christine Dawe had her first short story published at the age of ten, on the children's page of the *Liverpool Daily Post and Echo*. For this she received the princely fee of 10s. She was so delighted she immediately wrote another which was also accepted.

While in her teens, she continued to write features for arts and youth magazines, including one, illustrated by herself, concerning teenage fashions with some suggested improvements to school uniforms. Again, this was published by the *Echo*.

She also took the lead in many local drama productions. At fifteen she represented all Merseyside Youth Clubs by reading the Lesson at a ceremony in the Anglican Cathedral. She won several public speaking competitions and later became an adjudicator for the English Speaking Union public speaking contests. At Holly Lodge High School, West Derby, she won the Pilling Prize for Literature despite being the youngest entrant.

For eleven very happy years she taught A-Level English and Drama at a huge comprehensive school in Belle Vale, to adults and sixth-formers in the same class, plus English Comprehension to special needs groups. She then changed careers to

The author, aged twelve, a Oberon in *A Midsummer Night's Dream*.

take up acting and writing professionally. Recording the audio versions of full-length novels and biographies became her speciality, interspersed, for several years, with reading short stories on the BBC Radio Merseyside literary programme, *Write Now*. Her audio books include all of Helen Forrester's autobiographical saga, starting with *Tuppence to Cross the Mersey*. Although Christine narrates commentaries for travel documentaries, she also loves the fun of character voices for cartoons and computer games. On television, her appearances have included *Coronation Street*, *Brookside*, *Hollyoaks* and several commercials.

Using her previous experience in education, Christine has written books used in both senior and primary schools, some especially for reluctant teenage readers and others for the new citizenship subject in primary schools known as PSHE (Personal, Social and Health Education).

In memory of close family members, Christine supports the charities for Cancer Research, Kidney Research and the British Heart Foundation.

Cilla Black

'Hello Chuck, tell us yer name and where yer come from'

In 1960, when teenager Priscilla Maria Veronica White and her friends saved up enough money for a trip from Liverpool to North Wales, young Priscilla was delighted to see real cows and sheep at last. She had seen pictures of them before, but never the living animals. Quite a milestone in her life. But an even more important milestone was winning the talent competition at their destination, Butlins, Pwllheli, and being presented with the prize by a boy she had met several times before. His name was Richie Starkey, the drummer with Rory Storm and the Hurricanes. She always enjoyed his great sense of humour and in time they became good mates.

Ever since she was a toddler, Priscilla had loved music. Her mother had a beautiful soprano voice and could sing many operatic arias with ease. Her father was also musical. After work at the docks, he often played the harmonica during

Cilla Black with Phil Redmond and the cast of *Brookside*.

family sing-songs. He took great pride in his appearance and even more pride in his close-knit and loving family. When Priscilla was still a young child, she was encouraged to join in these informal gatherings. She soon realised that she loved being the centre of attention and developed an early ambition to become a professional singer. At this stage, she had no idea how to achieve this but she was determined to find a way.

First, she had to earn some money. On leaving school, she worked in the offices of BICC (British Insulated Calendar Cables) in Stanley Street. This brought two important advantages. As well as a reasonable salary enabling her to buy trendy jeans, colour shampoos for her hair and the occasional pop record from Nems music store, she was also entitled to a full lunch break. Being in the city centre was significant, too. It meant that she and her pals could dash to the nearby Cavern where the Beatles were alternating with other groups to play lunchtime concerts. Determined to become part of the Mersey Beat scene, and with her name now shortened to Cilla, she used her initiative and persuaded the manager of the Cavern that he needed a proper cloakroom with a check-out girl, instead of expecting fans to keep their wet and crumpled coats with them while screaming and leaping around to the music for an hour or more.

So she now had two jobs. Soon she had three. In the evenings, she became a waitress at the Zodiac coffee club. This helped her to mix with more of the up-and-coming stars from the music scene. On any free evenings she would go to hear the groups at the Blue Angel Club, in Seel Street.

Two separate events which were to shape the rest of her life happened almost simultaneously. Having wangled her way into singing occasional numbers at the Cavern, Cilla had become friendly with the Beatles. John would announce her, always jokingly pretending he couldn't pronounce her name properly. One night, he introduced her to the Beatles manager, Brian Epstein, saying, 'Brian, this is Cyril. She's the one to watch. You should sign her up.'

The second momentous encounter happened one evening at the Zodiac club. Cilla spotted an attractive new customer, blond, tanned and rather Scandinavian-looking. It wasn't long before the two got talking and Cilla was impressed by his chat-up lines. She soon discovered that most of this was just 'blarney', but by then she was totally smitten and the two became utterly devoted to each other. They never had eyes for anyone else from that moment onward. Bobby Willis and Cilla eventually married and, over the years to come, they had three sons.

Cilla's first audition for Brian Epstein was a disaster. The Beatles accompanied her rendition of 'Summertime', but they played it in their own key, not realising that Cilla needed a different pitch. Cilla then tensed up with nerves and Brian was unable to appreciate her talent. In 1963, when by chance he heard her again, he immediately realised her potential and drew up a contract for her – his only female client. After a misprint in a local music paper, Cilla found herself transformed into Cilla Black. As Cilla mentions in her autobiography, *Cilla*, although her father was disappointed at the change of surname, Epstein insisted on keeping it. Her friend

Richie Starkey also changed his name. After joining the Beatles, he became known as Ringo Starr.

Hit singles, television appearances and offers of representing the United Kingdom in the Eurovision Song Contest quickly flooded in. Cilla's version of 'Anyone Who Had A Heart' became an instant number one, the highest-selling single ever by a British female singer. Her records, nearly always about love, have stood the test of time and have been re-issued in album form several times. With her trim figure, fantastic legs and bubbly personality, Cilla was a natural for television stardom. Always fashion-conscious, she changed her image according to the trends. Musical crazes come and go, but Cilla adapted by turning herself into a chat show host and celebrity presenter. With Bobby's steadfast help as her business manager, Cilla's career soared to new heights. From 1984 to 2003, her programmes, including *Surprise, Surprise* and *Blind Date* drew enormous audiences and created many thousands of affectionate new fans. All over Britain, admirers became familiar with her Scouse phrases, such as 'A lorra, lorra laughs', and her warm-hearted introduction of any girl named Claire as 'Ar Clurr'.

Cilla turned down the chance of singing in the Eurovision Song Contest and at a later date she declined an offer of an Honorary Degree from John Moores University, Liverpool. This was owing to adverse comments from full-time students who didn't welcome the idea. But as the years went by, she was proud to receive the OBE as well as the award for best presenter from the Royal Television Society and the Lew Grade Award for the most popular programme on television. At last, in 2000, when invited to become a Fellow of John Moores University, Cilla was happy to accept and the ceremony took place at Liverpool's Anglican Cathedral.

For most of their married life, Cilla, Bobby and family lived in the manor house once owned by Sir Malcolm Sargent, the erstwhile principal conductor of the Royal Liverpool Philharmonic Orchestra. They celebrated their Pearl Wedding in the early part of 1999.

Cilla's song 'You're My World' must surely have been dedicated to her beloved husband who was her tower of strength until his untimely death late in 1999. Although devastated, Cilla continued hosting *Blind Date* for a while. When she felt she could no longer carry on, she made her surprise farewell, live on air. With the help of family and her very special friends, she later recuperated and regained her positive and optimistic outlook on life, and was happy to support Liverpool in 2008 – its year as Capital of Culture by starring in a pantomime at the huge Empire Theatre.

Alan Bleasdale

Jack of all trades; masterly and influential stage, screen and radio writer

Many people ask, 'How can I become a screenwriter, (author, poet, journalist?) What training do I need? What is the recipe for success?' The ingredients are simple. A wide experience of life, as many different kinds of jobs as possible, some foreign experiences and, above all, a deep understanding of human nature. All of these, plus supreme natural talent. Method: leave to

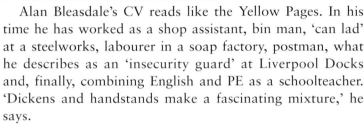

mature, blend together with determination and hard work. Perfect role model? Alan Bleasdale.

Alan Bleasdale's CV reads like the Yellow Pages. In his time he has worked as a shop assistant, bin man, 'can lad' at a steelworks, labourer in a soap factory, postman, what he describes as an 'insecurity guard' at Liverpool Docks and, finally, combining English and PE as a schoolteacher. 'Dickens and handstands make a fascinating mixture,' he says.

Huyton and Widnes were Alan's childhood haunts. His infant and junior school was St Aloysius, followed by Wade Deacon Grammar School, Widnes. His interest in sport provided a most enjoyable period during his session as team manager, with Eddie Kilshaw, at Huyton Boys football team, especially as the team won the English Schools Trophy in 1970/1. In fact, Alan regards it as one of his fondest memories.

'Teamwork', he says. 'You just can't beat it.'

This applies equally to his groundbreaking (in more ways than one) television series *The Boys from the Black Stuff*.

'Everything and everybody fell into place,' he continues. 'Everything I've ever done that has been any good has always involved other people. Otherwise, you might as well go off and be a novelist. Or even a hermit.'

In confirmation of this, Alan is keen to stress the strengths he has derived from a loving and supportive family. 'I wouldn't have had any so-called success without the backing of my parents, my wife and my children.'

Other people's children, particularly those suffering hardship, hold a special place in Alan's heart. He supports Steven Yip's charity KIND (Kids In Need and Distress) (see pp. 146–9) and he also takes a keen interest in Sahir House, a multi-cultural HIV support and information centre, linked with Liverpool's Hope University.

Modestly, Alan prefers not to name the many awards he has won, saying he prefers to leave mention to such things to fellow Liverpudlians with higher profiles than himself! But everyone knows that his awards are numerous and highly prestigious. His writing is always powerful, innovative and hugely influential, not least because of his darkly humorous style and full-blooded characterisations. After *Boys From The Black Stuff* gripped the nation's imagination, Yozzer's plaintively menacing demand, 'Gizza job. I can do that!' leapt into the English language and has stayed there ever since. The whole series had such far-reaching effects, it was repeated sooner than was usual, and most viewers were glad to watch it on both outings!

Scully was Alan's debut on television in 1975, having already been extremely well-received on radio. *Black Stuff* followed in 1982. Then, in 1986, came the dramatic *Monocled Mutineer*, starring Paul McGann, one of the four McGann brothers from the Liverpool television and theatrical dynasty. *GBH* again made a huge impact in 1991 and *Jake's Progress* reached Alan's devoted viewers in 1995. It was followed by Alan's own interpretation of Charles Dickens's *Oliver Twist*. In 2008, Alan's hilarious yet nail-biting comedy, *On the Ledge*, filled the newly resurgent Royal Court Theatre to capacity.

When writing or talking about his home town, Alan pulls no punches. He is a loving son of the city, one whose humour always shows through but who is not blind to the shortcomings of his 'ancestors' and 'siblings'. Let us allow him to sum up his philosophy in his own words, 'I've always thought that one great advantage to have as a writer, is the good fortune to be born and brought up somewhere interesting. You will note, for example, that there have been no truly notable or even vibrant writers from either Bognor Regis or Spital. And as you've probably gathered by now, I've lived almost all of my life in and around Liverpool. You should know straight away that I have no romantic illusions about Liverpool – parts of the city are still broken-down and run-down – it has considerable political and social problems – there are as many prats and pillocks in this city as there are anywhere else. Furthermore, we are a notoriously "last minute" city. At the time of writing, just weeks before the start of the celebrations of the City of Culture, it seems that "last second" city might be more appropriate'.

'However, Liverpool is also a fund of stories – a great gift to a writer. Sardonic humour and violence and genuine loud warmth all mixed together in a city that has been a league of nations for a very long time. It's usually a privilege to live in Liverpool. And, above all, you can't get too big-headed here – it's simply not allowed. For example, when there was all the fuss about *The Boys From The Black Stuff*, a lot of journalists came up from London to interview me. One such journalist got a cab from Lime Street station, and on the way, not being soft, he pumped the taxi driver about me, and what my work might mean to the people of Liverpool. I was lucky, and the driver was a fan, and he waxed lyrical all the way – apparently. Alan Bleasdale this and Alan Bleasdale that – all promise and fine adjectives – until the journalist got out of the cab at our house and said, "By the way, I'm actually meeting Alan Bleasdale now – I'll tell him what you were saying, if you want." The driver looked him straight in the eye and said, "Yer kiddin', aren't yer? Tell him from me – he can't f*****' write to save his life!"'

Good on yer, Alan! 'Nuff said!

Jean Boht

Winner of the 'Scousology Award' and many others

'The favourite period of my career? That's easy,' says Jean, 'Any time I'm working. I've been stage-struck from a very early age.' Jean was born in Bebington on the Wirral, close to Lord Leverhulme's Port Sunlight. Her infant and junior school days were spent at St Andrew's Primary, Bebington, followed by Wirral Grammar School For Girls.

'Both were important', says Jean. 'They both encouraged my "performing", from the age of five right through to sixteen. I showed off poems to the visiting vicar and wrote plays for myself. In my first year at grammar school, I played Elizabeth

Jean with her husband Carl Davis.

Bennett in *Pride and Prejudice*. This was wartime, remember, and frequently our lessons had to take place in bomb shelters. Fortunately, the staff were wonderful. I had a genius of a music teacher, Doris Parkinson. Every morning she would play a classical record in assembly. This was a treat, as in those days none of us had record players at home. "Parky" took us to concerts at the Philharmonic and opera at the Royal Court Theatre. The Art, English and History staff were excellent, too.'

Jean also enrolled at the Bedford School of Dancing and the Hillary Stafford-Burrows Dance School. From the age of thirteen, Jean appeared with the Birkenhead Operatic Society. This company had a very high reputation on Merseyside for the quality and professionalism of its productions, playing to packed houses in the enormous Royal Court and Empire theatres in Liverpool.

'I had a wonderful time,' recalls Jean. 'I ended up playing Nelly Forbush in *South Pacific.*'

'In those days,' she continues, 'the once-lovely Royal Court was the premier theatre in Liverpool, hosting major productions including the National Theatre and the Royal Shakespeare Company, and not the woebegone dump it is now. How sad that in this Year of Culture, there is nowhere in Liverpool for any London touring plays to be seen.' The Empire Theatre is ideal for spectacular shows, ballet and musicals but straight plays bypass Merseyside to find an audience at Theatr Clwyd, North Wales. 'We should be providing suitable experiences to encourage youngsters to enjoy theatre and think of it as part of their lifestyle,' insists Jean.

Jean's first professional job was in rep at the Liverpool Playhouse, for the princely salary of £1 per week, rising between 1961 and 1964 to stage manager, at £5 a week, while appearing in most productions as well, 'Usually playing old ladies. The "resident" old lady, Dulcie Bowman, had to leave suddenly to look after her sick husband so I took over all her parts.' In 1964, Jean went to London for a production of *St Joan of the Stockyards* at the Queens Theatre in the West End. After a season at Bristol's Old Vic, she returned to Liverpool for principal roles with John Hopkins, Lynda La Plante (Lynda Marchal in those days), Patrick Stewart and John Savident. 'The only drama training I ever had, was from David Scase, a most inspired director, and Philip Hedley who introduced us to the Stanislavsky method.' The year 1965 saw Jean at London's Royal Court, as well as the National Theatre and Joan Littlewood's Theatre Workshop.

'Television work came as a boon when I had children – easier than touring.'

Sons and Lovers, *Boys From The Black Stuff* and *Scully* were followed by *Some Mothers Do 'Ave 'Em* and *Last Of The Summer Wine*. Robin Nash directed Jean in Carla Lane's *I Woke Up One Morning* and *Bread*.

'This was to change my life for ever,' Jean recalls.

Ma Boswell, with her cordless phone tucked into her apron pocket, caught the nation's imagination and endeared Jean to family audiences everywhere. Presiding over the domestic trials and tribulations of the funniest dysfunctional tribe ever seen, Jean imbued the character with scatty affection and matriarchal devotion. Her memorable personification of the archetypal Scouse Mam, led to many West End engagements, to Chichester and to touring in Alan Bennett's *Monologues*. In 2006/7, Jean worked on six different films in Canada and New York, as well as appearing in *Holby City* and *The Bill*.

At one time, Jean was patron of twenty-seven charities.

At the moment her special interests are the British Homeopathic Association, Carla Lane's Animaline and the Jelly Bean Appeal at Wirral University Teaching Hospital, which aims to provide a relaxing environment for child patients. 'The A&E department is to be decorated as the interior of a yellow submarine,' says Debbie Green, Fund Raising Co-ordinator. 'Playstations and televisions are to be installed. We hope that residential areas can be provided for parents and siblings.' Jean also tries to find homes for racing dogs which have to retire at only five years of age. 'Such gentle creatures,' says Jean. 'They can make wonderful family pets.'

Jean was amazed and thrilled in 1989 when she was the subject of *This Is Your Life*. In the same year, another great joy was when Paul and Linda McCartney 'attended' Aveline's wedding in an episode of *Bread*.

Since their wedding in 1971, Jean and her composer/conductor husband, Carl Davis, have celebrated many years of happy marriage. Jean is justly proud of all her family; two daughters, Hannah who makes movies with husband David Law, and Jessie, who was in television administration until she and her cameraman husband, Richard Stevenson, started a family.

Jean won the best comedy actress award, the Variety Club Award and the Scousology Award (for local talent in aid of the BBC Children In Need appeal) for her appearances in *Bread*. She was also awarded an Honorary Fellowship by John Moores University.

Jean's mother, Teddy Dance, was also a remarkable lady in many ways; so much so that she warrants her own piece devoted especially to her (see p. 21).

Tony Booth

Proud to be a Scouse Git!

Tony Booth was born in Waterloo. He is a descendent of Algernon Booth whose nephew, John Wilkes Booth, shot President Abraham Lincoln. The Waterloo in question is situated on the outskirts of Liverpool, on the way to Southport.

Somewhere in this interesting lineage, a few fiery and unconventional genes have found their way into Anthony George Booth, the actor who became an overnight sensation along with Warren Mitchell in the BBC comedy series *'Til Death Us Do Part*. In this hugely popular sitcom, Tony's role was that of Mike Rawlins. But that is not the name by which Alf Garnett's son-in-law was so readily identified. Tony was universally recognised as the 'Scouse Git', a compliment, of course, to his convincing portrayal of that character and the way ardent admirers related to him. But Tony recalls a couple of incidents when fans obviously couldn't separate the actor from the character.

'I was driving along the motorway one day,' he says, 'when another car appeared behind me from nowhere. It stayed in the slow lane, right behind me but not attempting to overtake. The driver was tooting the horn for no reason. I couldn't make out what he wanted. There I was, in the slow lane, keeping to the speed limit. I wasn't preventing him from overtaking. So I wound down the window and signalled that he could overtake if he liked. At last, he moved into the middle lane and drove along beside me. His windows were open and he shouted across the carriageway, "Hiya, you Scouse Git. You alright?"

'Well, I though to myself, Johnny Speight, the writer and Denis Maine Wilson, the director, have made me so famous, people can even recognise the back of my head while driving at 65 miles an hour!'

'Another time,' he continues, 'I was walking along Lime Street in the centre of Liverpool, when a young feller shouted to me, "Alright, yer Scouse Git?" So I shouted back, "Hiya, yer Scouse Git. You alright?" he shot across the pavement, grabbed me by the throat and shoved me against the wall. "Don't you dare call me a Scouse Git," he roared at me. "But you started it. You called me a Scouse Git." "Yeah, but that's because you ARE a Scouse Git!" he growled. I didn't know whether to laugh or cry!'

Tony's first forays into the entertainment field took place during his National Service and from there he went into repertory theatre. Before long, parts in films and television began to materialise. Between 1960 and 1970, the saucy young adventurer type of character became popular. Tony's blond good looks made him an ideal candidate for the series of *Confessions* films, as the foil to Robin Askwith, the cheeky lad with the roving eye. Their spontaneous personalities and wicked charms brought assured success. For Tony, this was a mixed blessing. Plenty of enticing opportunities came his way and he was quick to take every advantage of short-lived dalliances. But long-term relationships and his first marriage suffered and slowly faded.

In *'Til Death Us Do Part*, Tony's continuous sparring with his screen father-in-law became the main feature of the series, despite the fact that Alf Garnett's bigoted views were, much against the writer's intentions, sometimes taken at face value and supported blindly by unthinking fans.

The strains of a long run can often be detrimental to an actor's health. Tony's contemporary, Richard Beckinsale, worked himself into an early grave. Many others fell by the wayside and had to give up the profession altogether. Tony found

solace in alcohol, until the inevitable happened: drink turned from support to slave-driver and Tony could no longer function without it. Demanding schedules, an unstable family life and a stormy temper, coupled with the effects of the grape and the grain began to shape his lifestyle.

Then came the terrible disaster which could so easily have resulted in his death. It happened one night in 1979 when Tony invited a couple of SAS men back to his flat. 'Because the door was locked, I decided to force an opening via the loft.' To gain entry, he piled up three drums of paraffin. Once he was inside, he heard an explosive sound 'like a whoooosh,' he says. He suddenly realised that flames were licking up all around him. In a panic, he screamed a warning to his wife of that time, Susie, and their daughters. Then he tried to escape but the exploding drums caused massive burns to his body and hands. He was in hospital for six months and had a total of twenty-six skin grafts. In the initial days of intensive care, he was declared clinically dead on three occasions. The only small mercy was that his face was spared. He says that throughout the whole of the six months, his eldest daughter, Cherie Blair, came to visit him every week without fail, consistently supporting him and helping him to build up the positive attitude that life was still worth living.

When at last able to leave hospital, he returned to Liverpool where his mother nursed him through the early stages of convalescence. In 1980, during the slow and painful recovery, Tony met up again with his long-time friend, the actress, Pat Phoenix. There had always been a deep affinity between them, dating back to their early days in show business. In the meantime, Patricia had become hugely popular as the icon Elsie Tanner in *Coronation Street*. Now that she was in a stable financial position, she invited Tony to live with her in her Cheshire home. In dressing his injuries and caring for him in every way, she continued his mother's good work and brought him back to a fitness he had never thought possible. After a blissful few years together, Pat's own health began to deteriorate. She had lung cancer. In 1986, when it became clear that Pat could not survive, she and Tony sealed their love by marrying in a Manchester hospital. A few days later, when Pat's death was announced, the whole nation was touched by the news of their tragic romance.

Tony has always had a flair for words and an engaging, if outrageous, charm. He has served as the president of the actors' union, Equity, and at one time used to campaign to further his son-in-law's political aspirations. Having canvassed on behalf of his daughter, Cherie, when she attempted to win a seat at Thanet, Booth then set about attending every possible by-election, telling voters that he had been specially sent by Tony Blair. These days, however, Booth questions the principles of Labour's foreign policy.

His connections with the ex-Prime Minister have caused Booth some wry smiles. On one occasion, when Tony Booth and his fourth wife, Stephanie, were living in Ireland, Tony wanted to send Christmas presents to his grandchildren, including the ones living at 10 Downing Street. When the Irish officials saw the famous address on the parcels, they over-reacted and subjected Booth to an embarrassing strip search. But years ago, when Booth was questioned for allegedly driving under the influence, he gave his address as 'The Palace of Westminster'! When asked to supply the name of his next of kin, he replied with all the dignity he could muster, 'The Prime Minister'!

In the final decade of the twentieth century and the early years of the twenty-first, Booth has shown his talents as a serious actor in several films, including the controversial *Priest*, as well as in the television soap operas *Eastenders* and *Emmerdale*. Having in the past appeared in *Coronation Street* but missed out on the Liverpool-based *Brookside*, Booth only needs a role in *Hollyoaks* to complete a neat quartet.

Cherie Blair and her sister Lyndsey are Tony's daughters from his first marriage to Gail. His other six daughters are from marriages and relationships with Julie, Susie and Stephanie.

In 1987, when Booth was travelling around Britain campaigning on behalf of the Labour Party, bedroom space at one location was in short supply. Tony had to share a bed with a colleague. Acutely aware of what the gossip columnists could make of such a situation, the two blokes lay in the darkness making a verbal list of all the women they could rely on as witnesses to their masculinity. Tony could have gone on until the early hours of the morning!

Bessie Braddock

Battling Bessie, the Poor Man's Friend (1899–1970)

Mention Liverpool and a few outstanding personalities immediately spring to mind. Whatever the list, the name Bessie Braddock is never missing. Born just before the turn of the twentieth century, this bouncing baby girl would grow up to live through at least part of the reigns of five monarchs, that is to say, the last two years of Victoria, then Edward VII, George V, Edward VIII, George VI and Elizabeth II.

Bessie, however, had no time for the trappings of royalty. She was interested only in improving the quality of life for the lowest-earners of British society. From the very start of her life, Bessie was involved in politics. Her mother, Mary Bamber, had always had a strong and genuine commitment to social reform and to improving working conditions. Giving birth to Bessie certainly wasn't going to keep her at home when there was important work to be done. Only three weeks after Bessie was born, her mother carried her to a union meeting. No doubt there was a moment when baby Bessie used her healthy lungs to make her presence known, especially if she needed feeding.

That healthy pair of lungs and strident voice were to be used in public time and time again as the years went by. An indication of Bessie's natural flair for oratory showed itself when Bessie, aged nine, recited a long poem before a large audience at a Labour meeting in Sun Hall, Kensington. Her practical help for the poor also started at an early age. As a child, encouraged by her parents, Bessie often joined her mother outside the imposing St George's Hall to help with the soup kitchen. Bessie would ladle broth into bowls for the lean, dispirited and poverty-stricken of the area. Although it was now the twentieth century, many homes still had no running water and the women market traders still wrapped themselves in black, hand-knitted shawls to keep out the cold. Mother and twelve-year-old daughter were both present, once again outside St George's Hall, on 'Bloody Sunday' in 1911, when police charged at the hundreds of striking transport workers who had gathered peacefully to hear Tom Mann address them.

Bessie grew up with only one aim in mind, to raise the living conditions of her townsfolk. At first, she thought her route to achieving this ambition was via the Communist Party. It wasn't long, however, before she became disillusioned. She lost patience when she realised that everything seemed to be dictated by faraway Russia, leaving no room for decisions by those who were closely involved in local situations. She was just as resentful of the hierarchy in Moscow as she was with those in London. She claimed, 'The Communist Party hates social democracy even more than it hates the Tories.'

So in 1926 she joined the Labour Party instead, and soon became a member of the Liverpool Council, representing St Anne's Ward. Here she was vociferous in her

Bessie dancing with a male nurse at a hospital function.

campaigning. Determined to be heard above all others, she once smuggled a powerful megaphone into a debate to amplify her criticism and demands about poor housing conditions. She didn't really need a megaphone to draw attention to herself. She was a big person with a big personality. She soon became 'The Poor Man's Friend' to admirers and fiery 'Battling Bessie' to her opponents. She proudly called herself 'a rebel'.

She met and married kindred spirit Jack Braddock in 1922. They first lived in Freehold Street in Fairfield, later moving to Zig-Zag Road, West Derby, so named because of its Z-shaped twists and angles. Jack was also a councillor and became Leader of the Council in 1955.

As well as becoming a union leader, President of the Liverpool Trades Council and later the first female Labour MP for Liverpool, Bessie still found time to join the ambulance service during the Second World War. In parliament, Bessie took up the causes for better conditions in prisons and mental institutions, something that few others bothered about in those days. She often flouted etiquette, tradition and chauvinism. In the House of Commons in 1947, during a debate on the Transport Bill, all the Tory MPs walked out in protest. So that her colleague, the Minister of Transport, didn't have the embarrassment of addressing an empty Chamber, Bessie got up and jokingly changed over to the opposition benches. The story grew out of all proportion and she was accused of bringing the House into disrepute by 'dancing an Irish jig'. Her weight and solid figure would have made this somewhat difficult! Although she tried her best, this difficulty in keeping her figure under control caused a problem in the austerity years after the war. The fashions of the time were unflattering to all women and outsize ladies couldn't find anything to suit or fit them. Once again, Bessie took up the cause and even joined in a fashion parade of designs suitable for larger matrons.

In 1956, concerned about teenage louts shooting off air rifles, the fearless firebrand herself confiscated three of them and took the weapons into the Commons. In character with her dramatic personality, she triggered them off towards the ceiling. She then crossed the floor and handed them to the Home Secretary and quietly allowed herself to be escorted from the chamber.

She never minced her words, often calling her opponents 'rats' or 'outright liars' or threatening them that 'I'd like to take a machine-gun to the lot of you!'

This, coupled with her strict moral code and her lack of conventional beauty did nothing to endear her to her adversaries. As she never drank nor smoked, she found fault with Winston Churchill on one occasion when she loudly attested, 'Mr Churchill, you are drunk!' His reply reverberated around the corridors of Parliament 'Yes, Mrs Braddock and you are ugly! But tomorrow I shall be sober!'

Mrs Braddock and Lady Astor share the honours as far as the attribution of another anecdote about Churchill is concerned. The exasperated lady exclaimed, 'If you were my husband I'd serve you poison!' to which the reply was, 'Madam, if I were your husband, I'd drink it!'

However, joking aside, Churchill must have valued Bessie's integrity because in 1954, he invited her to sit on the Royal Commission for Mental Health, one of the causes dear to her heart.

In 1964, Jack and Bessie wrote their joint autobiography, *The Braddocks*.

In 2001, Betty Boothroyd, then speaker of the House of Commons, unveiled a Blue Plaque over the front door of Bessie's former home in Zig-Zag Road to commemorate this long-serving crusader.

Jamie Carragher

Liverpool's Home-Grown Pride –
and Proud of it

So popular is the stalwart Jamie Carragher that, to the tune of the Beatles' famous 'Yellow Submarine,' the Liverpool FC fans sing out, 'We all dream of a team of Carraghers, a team of Carraghers, a team of Carraghers.' The unassuming Jamie appreciates the compliment but reminds the Kopites that a team of defenders isn't likely to score many goals.

Six foot of strength, speed and all-round capability, James Lee Duncan Carragher was born in Bootle, Merseyside, and has been the backbone of the Reds and their best kept secret since the 1996/7 season. It is difficult to believe he was a childhood supporter of Everton. Since his first appearance at Anfield, his loyalty has never wavered. His first outing in the big boys' League Cup was as substitute for right-back Rob Jones. Then, within ten days, as a midfielder, filling in for John Barnes, he showed his true worth, scoring the first goal in the 3–0 win against Aston Villa.

As part of the England Under-21 team, in 1997/8 he played in twenty-seven matches earning him the title of most-capped Under-21 player. His rise into the England senior team came in 1999 against Hungary. Back at Liverpool, despite the Reds' defeat in the UEFA Cup against Celta Vigo in Spain, Jamie's place in central defence was never in question, as he gave a steadfast display of his unwavering personal dedication. His concentration has always been unfaltering, his tenacity an example to all and his power as a defender would be a huge benefit to any goalkeeper. He has even denied chances to the likes of David Beckham and Barcelona's Luis Enrique.

A broken leg was to veto his chances during most of 2003/4 but, undeterred, he returned to the first team demonstrating his unyielding perseverance, especially when manager Rafa Benitez arrived on the scene and decided Jamie could show his mettle in central defence. Once encouraged to use his natural talent and constructive aptitude, 'Carra' proved to be a crowd-pleaser with true international quality. In 2005, Liverpool's triumph in the UEFA Champions League was due in no small part to Carragher's skill and dogged determination. Despite suffering from cramp, he lit up the last few minutes of extra time with two priceless interceptions, helping to assure him of the Player of the Year title.

In 2005, Jamie pledged his allegiance to Liverpool by signing a four-year contract and shortly afterwards scored his first goal in six years. Exactly one month later, when he stood in as captain for the injured Steven Gerrard, he lifted the UEFA Super Cup after the victory over CSKA Moscow.

The year 2006 brought two vastly contrasting moments in Jamie's career. In the World Cup quarter-finals against Portugal in July, he scored with his first attempt in the shoot-out, only to have it disallowed by the ref who had not yet blown his whistle. Frustratingly, Carra's second effort was blocked by the Portuguese keeper,

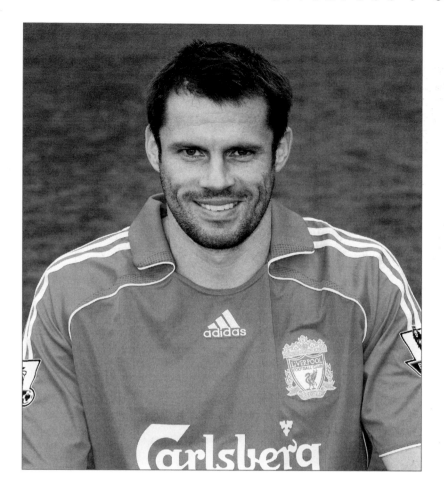

Ricardo Pereira. Though Jamie is not a prolific goalscorer, fortunately, in December of that year he redeemed himself with panache. The Kop went wild with delight when he sent the ball skimming under Fulham's goalie, Jan Lastuvka.

Although Jamie decided to retire from international matches, citing his disappointment that successive managers had not picked him at centre-back, he had set a record for the most appearances in European competition for Liverpool. In May 2007 he was named Man Of The Match and followed this with being voted Liverpool's Player of the Year, 2006/7. In June 2007, he signed a deal keeping him with Liverpool until 2011.

Off the field, happily married to his childhood sweetheart and with two children, Jamie has a social conscience, demonstrated by his agreeing to appear in television star Samantha Janus's anti-bullying video, *Stand Tall*. Because he is respected as a genuine Mr Nice Guy by the youngsters among his legion of fans, and is regarded as a true influence for the good of today's teenagers, Jamie has been awarded the Freedom of the Borough of Sefton, Merseyside.

The Exceptional Family of Bishop Chavasse 1846–1928

With Special Reference to Noel Chavasse – Doctor, Sweetheart, Hero (1884–1917)

In the days before the expression, 'dysfunctional family' was in such constant use, one of the most functional families Liverpool has ever known was that of Bishop Francis Chavasse, his affectionate and supportive wife, Edith, and their seven children. Added to these, mention must be made of the bishop's brother, Thomas, and his family, especially his son, Arthur. The bishop's sister and her husband the Revd Henry Squires had a son, Francis, who is part of this story. Edith's nephew, Louis, also deserves a place in this remarkable saga.

All of these gallant kinsmen proved to be the stuff that legends are made of. Woven through the story of this dynasty are two heraldic threads, one of commitment to the Hippocratic Oath, the other of bravery and devotion to duty. In various ways, they all served their fellow men in the First World War and four of them gave their lives for their country. Between them, numerous medals were won.

The seven children of Francis and Edith Chavasse were all born while Francis was still Rector of St Peter-le-Bailey in Oxford. First-born was Dorothea, followed by identical twin boys, Christopher and Noel, born in 1884. These two struggled valiantly from the moment they were born. For their first month it was never sure whether they would survive. Then, in less than a year, they nearly died from an attack of typhoid fever. Next came another pair of twins, this time girls, Marjorie and May. The remaining two boys, Bernard and Aiden, followed at two-yearly intervals.

With the very best of parental guidance and examples of unprecedented generosity to others, the family unit became spontaneously loving, happy, honourable, devoted to each other, devout in their attitude towards religion and the service of mankind, and hardworking in every way.

The children were educated at home until the age of twelve. After that Noel and Christopher attended Magdalen College School in Oxford, as day boys. Neither were very robust but they did enjoy sports and athletics. In 1900, their father was appointed Bishop of Liverpool. The whole family had to move away from their genteel, academic surroundings to the harsh reality of northern England in the final year of Queen Victoria's reign. They took up residence at 19 Abercromby Square, close to the centre of Liverpool. This brought them nearer to the bishop's brother, Dr Thomas Chavasse, his wife and children, Gwen, Arthur, Gladys and Esme in North Wales. The two families often visited each other. At that time there was no cathedral in Liverpool. The new bishop developed a great longing to provide the diocese with an edifice of suitable stature and beauty. Noel and Christopher were enrolled at Liverpool College and continued with their sporting interests as well as their preparation for university entrance. Here, they also came into contact with the battalion of the Liverpool Scottish, which influenced Noel's choice of unit later in life.

In 1904, Noel and Christopher returned to Oxford to study at Trinity College. The following year, there was much celebration when the bishop's brother Dr Thomas Chavasse received a knighthood for his services to medicine and, only one year later, the bishop was able to see his dreams beginning to take shape when a twenty-two-year-old Roman Catholic architect, Gilbert Scott, later knighted, won the right to design the monumental Gothic-style cathedral. The foundation stone was laid by King Edward VII and Queen Alexandra.

These happy occasions brought the young cousins together and Noel became particularly friendly with his Uncle Tom's daughter, Gladys.

It is a testament to the open-mindedness of Liverpool dignitaries that the Anglican Cathedral was designed by a Catholic and the original architect of the Catholic Cathedral was a Protestant, Sir Edwin Lutyens. The two fine twentieth-century buildings are joined by a short road called Hope Street.

Twin brothers, Christopher and Noel, had successfully completed their degree courses by 1909. Noel joined the Liverpool Medical School in Brownlow Hill. He then moved on to the Liverpool Southern Hospital. Here he received great encouragement from Sir Robert Jones, the esteemed orthopaedic surgeon, to whom Noel subsequently became house surgeon (see Sir Robert Jones, p. 66). It was in 1910 that Noel passed the primary exam of the Royal College of Surgeons. Christopher took a different path in life and trained as a minister of the church. It was also in 1910 that he was ordained by his father in St Bride's Church, Catherine Street. He then became a curate in St Helens. In 1913, Christopher became chaplain to the Fourth Army Corps. He was posted to St Nazaire and then to Rouen in France. Very shortly afterwards Noel joined the Liverpool Scottish Regiment.

Noel Chavasse, VC.

When war broke out and Noel was posted to Belgium, his naturally easy-going and friendly personality made him immediately popular with his fellow officers and equally so with the other ranks. Throughout every battle, Noel was kind, efficient and extremely sympathetic to the wounded men he treated. He was way ahead of his time in realising that the trauma of violent combat could cause psychological as well as physical damage. Intuitively, he knew that men who were suffering from deep and sudden shock were neither cowards nor malingerers. Some of the sights and conditions these young and naïve boys experienced were beyond human endurance. No wonder their minds, as well as their battered bodies, could not cope. Conditions, of course, were atrocious. With the flooded trenches and the icy weather, the lack of proper protective footwear and kilts instead of trousers for the Liverpool Scottish were ill-suited for trench warfare. Worse was to come. Trenchfoot led to gangrene and the poor conditions caused stomach upsets, all adding to the agony of wounds received from the enemy.

Although Noel and Christopher did have occasional leave when they were able to meet up with each other or visit Blighty, most of Noel's days were a constant struggle to patch up the young soldiers around him. The two youngest brothers, Bernard and Aiden, also enrolled for duty and served valiantly in Europe. Their sister May volunteered to help with nursing in France. Dorothea, the eldest, already married to a vicar, with a family of her own, headed a committee supplying hand-knitted socks, scarves and gloves, as well as chocolate and other luxuries to the troops. Marjorie did as much war work as she could while caring for their ailing mother. Their aunt, Thomas's wife Frances, opened a convalescent home for wounded soldiers. She was so highly regarded, she was awarded the MBE. Her own daughters and the bishop's daughters all nursed there at various times. Her son Arthur, also a doctor, served in northern France. Young Francis Chavasse Squires became a captain in the Third Sikh Pioneers. All were patriotic and constantly looking for ways to support each other and the wider community.

Among other battlegrounds Noel served in Ypres and Passchendaele, two of the most notorious hell-holes of the First World War, all the time operating under the most difficult conditions and perilously close to the front line. All around him were the casualties of shelling and snipers' bullets. Iodine and carbolic soap were in constant demand. Food was meagre and tasteless. Lice were an ever-present irritation. Sir Robert Jones still corresponded with Noel, sending practical advice and encouragement. Noel also received letters from his cousin, Gladys. She was especially pleased to hear that he had been awarded the Military Cross.

Then dreadful news arrived that cousin Captain Frances Squires, aged thirty, had been killed in Aden. He was posthumously awarded the Military Cross. Everyone was shocked into realising the real horrors of war.

In his rare moments of quietness, Noel dreamed of peace, home and the possibility of marriage. Between bouts of active service, he managed to meet up with Gladys and realised that he was falling in love with her. He was so modest, however, that he wasn't sure if he was good enough for her. So he failed to declare his feelings openly until much later and then not directly, only in a letter after encouragement from his sister.

Noel was not a natural horseman but riding was a speedy way of reaching his patients. He often went out single-handed searching for wounded. He wouldn't give up until he had assured himself that no wounded were left behind. On his return, exhausted already, he would do everything possible to clean up the injuries, disinfect them, operate, then stitch and dress them. All this was done under the most primitive conditions. One of his 'hospitals' consisted of a dugout that he himself had excavated. The cellar of a ruined building was the convalescent home. His own bed at that time was improvised from a broken stretcher. Naturally, before long he was promoted to captain.

Field ambulances were notoriously unreliable and inadequately stocked. On one occasion, in a moonlit wood almost denuded by shellfire, the muddy ground littered with hundreds of allied and enemy dead, he found one young soldier clinging to life with his arm so intensely damaged that there was only one way to save him. There and then, the equally young doctor, up to his knees in the quagmire, had to cut away the remnants of the shattered arm with scissors. The operation was lit only by the moon and a torch held by Noel's stretcher-bearer. Only after the operation was complete was it possible to slosh back to base, carrying their blood-spattered burden, taking two hours just to reach the edge of the wood. This was only one example of Noel's devotion to his fellow men. His charisma is proved by the fact that he later persuaded a German prisoner of war, who was an excellently qualified doctor, to minister to British casualties as caringly as he would to his own patients.

The dead and wounded were not only nameless strangers. Tragedy struck again when Gladys's brother, Dr Arthur Chavasse, died in Le Havre. Pneumonia was the immediate cause but ultimately, of course, it was the result of the conditions under which the young doctor was compelled to work. Gladys and all her family were distraught. Noel was unable to be with his beloved cousin and could only write to send his heartfelt sympathy.

There are many other examples of Noel's selfless devotion to his fellow men. As well as the hundreds who were brought to his makeshift dressing stations at the various battlegrounds throughout the war, Noel frequently ministered to the injured actually within sight of the enemy, even while the attack was still raging all around him. Many a time bullets missed him by inches. With such instant repairs to wounds, he single-handedly saved untold numbers of lives and rescued more from what would otherwise have been hours of agonising pain, lying in the mud. No matter where he was posted, he always worked tirelessly, staunching blood, patching damaged tissue, providing splints for shattered bones. Never once did he take heed for his own safety. His courage and cheeriness became legendary. His patients came to regard him as a lucky charm, and a sure sign of their eventual recovery. He seemed permanently oblivious to danger.

It was in October 1916 that Captain Noel Chavasse was again honoured. This time with the Victoria Cross. Not only was his sweetheart, Gladys, thrilled and delighted and his family proud beyond words, but Liverpool and indeed the whole country claimed him as a hero, a pin-up in fact. Cigarette cards, a favourite collectors' item in those days, featured his portrait and he received shoals of congratulations by letter and telegram. There were celebrations everywhere, even in a chateau near Ypres where a dinner was held in Noel's honour. Some time later, the twice-decorated doctor was welcomed home by the ecstatic Gladys and by his own parents. To everyone's delight, Noel and Gladys became officially engaged. Noel returned to duty. The actual investiture didn't take place until the following February. Now that Noel had both MC and VC after his name, his father rightly predicted, 'Until now, you have always been known as the son of the Bishop of Liverpool. From now on I shall be known as the father of Captain Chavasse.'

There was no let-up, however, and Noel returned yet again to the theatre of war and his makeshift operating theatre. He turned down an offer of being posted to a quieter area where there was an orthopaedic surgery in need of his skills. He felt that he was still needed at the front line. Where ever there was heavy fighting, that was where his immediate help should be.

The rollercoaster of emotions brought terrible sadness again, when Mrs Chavasse's nephew, Louis, was killed in action on the Somme. He had been a bright, happy and very popular young man.

In 1917, Gladys showed her own bravery and determination. She was so much in love with her young hero that she obtained a special marriage licence, then applied to work in a voluntary canteen in Paris, intending to reach her fiancé somehow and to marry him in spite of the continuing war.

Noel's brothers were also courageous. Aiden was wounded and reported missing, presumed dead. Bernard, a medical officer, happened to be in the vicinity at the time. Ignoring his own safety, he tried desperately to locate his youngest brother. Bernard was later awarded the Military Cross for bravery. Christopher also performed many acts of valour and received the Military Cross for his bravery and his services as a padre.

In 1917, as the battles raged on, Noel was able to discover a huge dugout built and previously used by the enemy. This saved precious time and effort as Noel was needed immediately just as another attack began. The gallant doctor stood up and waved to his comrades to indicate where this first-aid post was now situated. In doing so, he took a hit on the head by shrapnel. Others dressed the wound for him as best they could. He continued under great duress to attend to his fellow men working late into the night. The following day the battle raged on, the devil rain returned, flooding the trenches yet again. Food and drinking water were once more in short supply. The allies were now gaining ground, but injuries were still severe. Although wounded himself, the brave young doctor continued cleaning and dressing the broken and bleeding bodies brought to him on the stretchers. Somehow Noel suffered another injury and yet he wouldn't give in. In the confusion, details were scarce but the following night the explosion of a shell was so close that Noel was again violently injured. Within a couple of days, he sustained four different injuries, the worst causing unspeakable pain and damage to his vital organs. The blood flowing into the mud of the first-aid trench was now mostly Noel's. He wouldn't accept help. Instead he sent out the survivors to bring back more wounded comrades. Eventually Noel was transferred to hospital where he was operated on. Still showing magnificent fortitude, he remained cheerful and optimistic, determined to recover. But the time came when he needed strong doses of pain-killing morphine. No matter what was done to alleviate his suffering it was all to no avail. The gaping hole in his abdomen would not heal. He died on the third anniversary of the outbreak of the First World War. Heartbroken Gladys hid her agonising sorrow by devoting herself to further war work.

Posthumously, Noel was again honoured with the Victoria Cross. Two VCs, known as the VC and Bar. A photograph of Dr Noel Chavasse now has pride of place in the Liverpool Medical Institution.

A park near Liverpool's famous waterfront now bears the name Chavasse Park. There is hope that a statue of Noel Chavasse, Captain and Doctor, will soon grace that area. It is to be hoped that the other members of his extended family will also be commemorated.

Teddy Dance

Pianist for Charity – Busker Extraordinaire

Jean Boht's mother, Teddy Dance was a famous figure in Liverpool's city centre. Not far from the scruffy, hippy-style guitarists, buskers and mouth-organ players squatting on the pavement, this elegant and mature lady sat regally upright at a quality piano, between the main branch of Marks & Spencer's and George Henry Lee's, an upmarket department store now part of the John Lewis chain. From spring to autumn, for four consecutive years, shoppers were delighted by selections of popular and classical music, expertly played on a superior instrument by this charming and friendly lady.

Teddy Dance raised over £56,000 towards a scanner for Clatterbridge Hospital, the leading hospital on Merseyside for the treatment of cancer. The piano arrived each morning and was put to bed when the shops closed, courtesy of the 'boys' from Rushworth's Music Store. As the crow flies, this is not far from Teddy's solo 'stage' near the Playhouse Theatre. But pushing a full-sized piano around two corners and slightly uphill, every day, was a feat in itself.

Teddy was self-taught. She left school at the age of twelve. 'She learned tonic solfa, Doh, Re, Me, etc.,' says Jean. 'Then, hearing the tunes in her head, she sat at the kitchen table to write down the notes to use at a later date, when she could find a real instrument.' As well as this, Teddy learned and later taught ballroom dancing, specialising in the Charleston. 'She was much loved by everyone who knew her,' continues Jean, 'and I consider her an absolute genius.' Certainly all who heard her and contributed to her charity, remember her with great admiration and affection. What a unique and enterprising thing to do. And all for the good of others.

Teddy's husband Bertie had the advantage of a more formal education with real music lessons but taught himself to play the accordion. As well as Jean, Mr and Mrs Dance had another talented daughter, Maureen. During the Second World War, the family formed an act to entertain patients in hospitals and also at Army and RAF camps all over Merseyside. Maureen is also gifted musically. In adult life she took the lead in *Guys and Dolls*, singing with supreme ease in the huge Royal Court Theatre, Liverpool. As children, in the family concert party, it was their mother Teddy who encouraged both daughters to develop their natural abilities. Teddy's grandchildren have all inherited her interest in entertainment. As well as Jean's and Carl's daughters mentioned previously, Maureen's son, Stephen Noonan, has appeared many times on television and in the theatre.

In honour and memory of Teddy's amazing charitable fundraising and musical flair, there is an engraved paving stone commemorating the spot in Liverpool city centre where Teddy dedicated so much of her time and talent to the benefit of others.

Carl Davis

Cosmopolitan Composer, Conductor and Contributor to Liverpool's Culture

O f course, it all started with the amazing imagination of Jane Austen, but to bring her *Pride and Prejudice* to life in the twentieth century, it needed the input of Andrew Davies who adapted the novel for the small screen, the cast who epitomised the characters so perfectly and, not least, Carl Davis who composed such superbly apt theme music.

Since 1961, the prolific Carl Davis has been a much-loved and revered adopted son of Liverpool. Although he was born in New York and retains his American accent, his affinity with Liverpool is deep and abiding. He regards Britain as his spiritual home, and has been happily married to Liverpudlian actress Jean Boht for many years.

Highly esteemed in the world of classical music, Carl's work takes him all round the globe for guest appearances as visiting conductor. In addition, he conducts the London Philharmonic Orchestra and returns frequently to conduct the Royal Liverpool Philharmonic Orchestra. He also has a mission to make music accessible, enjoyable and popular for everyone. He feels that it should not be elitist, appealing to only a few *cognoscenti*. To this end, he created the Liverpool Pops. In recent summers, a huge marquee-style auditorium has drawn audiences of thousands to its waterfront venue on Merseyside's vast Albert Dock car park, to attend Carl's immensely popular concerts. In these, he introduces an eclectic mixture of classical and light music, often drawing attention to the numerous films, television programmes and commercial advertisements which use the symphonies of 'the old masters' for their background themes. These include everything from Hovis Bread and British Airways to Cyril Abraham's Liverpool shipping saga, *The Onedin Line* and football's World Cup in Germany in 2006.

Another of Carl's strong affiliations with Liverpool is his friendship with Sir Paul McCartney. The two joined forces in 1991, to compose the *Liverpool Oratorio*, premiered at the Liverpool Anglican Cathedral, conducted, of course, by Carl. Dame Kiri Te Kanawa, Sir Willard White, Sally Burgess and Terry Hadley were the soloists with the support of the cathedral's superb choir. This impressive choral work marked the celebration of the Royal Liverpool Philharmonic Orchestra's 150th birthday and has subsequently been performed worldwide.

John Thaw, so strongly associated with *Inspector Morse*, diversified into a serialised television drama set in war-torn London and the surrounding countryside. *Goodnight Mr Tom* benefited not only from a strong cast and an appealing storyline, but also from the appropriately evocative composition of Carl's background music. Carl's other themes include *The Far Pavilions*, *The Snow Goose*, *The Naked Civil Servant*, *Cranford* and the 1960s satirical comedy series that made stars of Ronnie Barker, Ronnie Corbett and John Cleese, *That Was The*

Week That Was. He also wrote three stories for orchestra with Carla Lane. *The Town Fox and Other Tales* were recorded by the cast of Carla's sitcom, *Bread.*

Clever and innovative uses of original music constitute Carl's modern accompaniments to vintage silent films. The movies of Charlie Chaplin, Harold Lloyd and Buster Keaton have benefited from a revival, thanks to a fresh approach from Carl's scores, played live in cinemas by the Liverpool Philharmonic Orchestra with Carl conducting.

Modern films, *The French Lieutenant's Woman, Topsy Turvy, Scandal, Champions* and the D.H. Lawrence story, *The Rainbow* all owe their musical appeal to Carl's imaginative compositions.

Ballet, of course, cannot exist without music and here Carl also shines. His creativity has enhanced productions of the Scottish Ballet, the Birmingham Royal Ballet, the Northern Ballet, the English National Ballet, Sadler's Wells and Ballet Central. The subjects for these dance presentations have varied between *Aladdin, Alice In Wonderland, A Christmas Carol, Cyrano de Bergerac* and the life and paintings of the Salford artist, L.S. Lowry.

Sir Willard White, the magnificent American bass-baritone has sung on Carl's recent CD release for the festive season and the BBC keeps re-inviting Carl to record more series of his radio programme, *Carl Davis Classics.* In 2005, Carl was honoured with the CBE. He has also received the Chevalier des Arts et des Lettres from the French Minister of Culture.

The world is fortunate that Carl's career spans parts of the twentieth and twenty-first centuries. Naturally, there have been many geniuses in the field of musical inspiration. But most of the great composers were seen and heard by only a limited number of aficionados, always live, of course. Thanks to the magical technology of film, video, CD and DVD, Carl's charismatic personality and his prolific diversity have been captured for many generations to come, as well as for his friends and admirers, and his brothers and sisters on Merseyside.

William Ralph Dean 1907–80

Dixie Dean: The Best Ever for Everton

The word most associated with this all-time best and most prolific goalscorer in English football history? Legendary. Some of the facts about Dixie Dean's achievements are so incredible that the song, 'Is it true what they say about Dixie?' might almost have been written in his honour.

When he was born in Birkenhead in 1907, his parents had been married for fifteen years and already had four children, all girls. After William was born, there were two more daughters. Fortunately, although Mr and Mrs Dean were mature parents, they both lived to be ninety, so they were able to bask in the reflected glory of their unparalleled son.

From a very early age, William loved football. His father was a devoted Everton fan, and as soon as he took young William to a match the die was cast. In this case, the 'dye' was bright blue accompanied by dazzling white.

At the age of eleven, William went to a Borstal corrective school for wayward boys. He wasn't sent there. He went because he wanted to. The Borstal in question was actually called the Albert Industrial School for Young Delinquents. William asked to go there because it had much better sporting amenities than his own Laird Street School. Money at home was scarce, so William used to get up at four in the morning to help the milkman. As well as pocket money, the bonus was that lifting heavy crates and churns helped to strengthen his muscles. Before he started playing in formal teams, William used to go to the local park for a kick-about with his pals. As he was responsible for looking after his baby sister, her pram often became a makeshift goalpost, the other being a sturdy tree. Once, William was so engrossed with the game that when evening came and all the lads sprinted home together, William suddenly realised he had left the pram and its contents behind. His sprint became a dash to rescue the baby and then a stroll home, whistling as if nothing had happened.

While he was still a schoolboy, young Dean began to be accepted, even sought after by men's teams. He played for the Wirral clubs of Pensby and then Tranmere Rovers, earning the very favourable figure of £4 10s a week. It was at about this time that he somehow acquired the nickname that became world famous. 'Dixie Dean' tripped off the tongue more easily than William or even Bill. Although he never liked it, that is how he will always be remembered.

Many clubs could see that he was a rising star but it was Everton that Dixie wanted to join. The Blues paid a £3,000 transfer fee for him and rumour has it that he only received £30 of that. Even that was donated by his mother to a local hospital.

Dixie soon gained a reputation for his fantastic headers and great goalscoring ability. Now a successful professional, he could afford a motorbike. On a non-training day, he invited his girlfriend on a trip to nearby North Wales. On the way to St Asaph, they were involved in a serious accident with another motorcycle carrying two men. The young lady escaped relatively unhurt but all three men were critically injured. Dixie was rushed to hospital with a fractured skull and a broken jaw. Immediate life-saving surgery was needed. It was touch and go whether he would survive. Apocryphal stories exist as to whether a metal plate was inserted into his skull, some saying that this was the initial procedure and that the plate was subsequently removed. But why two such dangerous operations would be performed is debatable. Whatever the truth of the matter, doctors were certain that Dean would never play football again. It was only when, during convalescence, Dixie climbed several fruit trees to pick apples for nurses and fellow patients, that one startled doctor pronounced him fit enough to resume training. When Dixie returned to his phenomenal goalscoring, many of these being headers, fans and opponents began to believe there was something akin to a fantasy hero about him and the rumours about the metal plate increased. It wasn't only his remarkable headers that put him in a class of his own. His speed, fancy footwork and instinctive way of creating goals for his team mates were also extraordinary. In the slump years of a recession, Merseysiders were so grateful for the magic he brought to their Saturdays that he became their idol.

As a role model too, he set a superb example. During his whole career, this original 'Mr Nice Guy' was never booked or sent off. He was certainly more sinned against than sinner. One particularly vicious tackle caused him the loss of one testicle. The agony can only be imagined.

In a dazzling career, one year shines even brighter than all others. During the 1927/8 season, Dixie Dean played in thirty-nine of Everton's league matches. In every game he had been building up his goalscoring total. A record of sixty goals in one season was the aim. As injury curtailed his chances in one of the matches and he missed another while playing for England, the final game of the year seemed to bring little hope of the longed-for aggregate. Just as everyone was resigned to the fact that the impossible really was impossible, with only five minutes to go, the incredible happened. Heading the ball into the net, Dixie Dean had scored sixty goals for the Toffees in one sensational season, causing the loudest and longest standing ovation Goodison Park has ever known. Standing? More like jumping up and down, hugging strangers, cheering and exploding with joy. The match could not be resumed for what seemed like an eternity of delirious excitement. His record has never been broken.

Dixie's perfect headers are even more remarkable when you consider that footballs in those days were made of leather. In rainy weather, these would soak up water and become extremely heavy. To fortify himself, Dean had a favourite little tipple. Before each game he would take two raw eggs whisked up in a small glass of sherry. It certainly worked for him!

In 1931, he married Ethel Fossard and they later had three sons and a daughter. By 1933, when he was team captain, earning £8 a week, he led the Blues to victory at Wembley. In total he won sixteen England caps and was one of the very first players to wear a numbered shirt, choosing the number nine. During his lifetime he won the Sunday Pictorial Trophy for sixty league goals in one season, Lewis's Medal to commemorate 200 league goals in a hundred and 99 appearances, the Hall of Fame trophy and the FA Writers' Association inscribed Silver Salver.

After retirement, he managed a pub in Chester. In later years, the amputation of a leg necessitated the use of a wheelchair but this didn't keep him away from Goodison Park. He was watching the end of a derby match between Everton and Liverpool when he collapsed and died from a heart attack.

That was in 1980 but his name and fame live on. In 2001, Everton Chairman Bill Kenwright commissioned the statue that now stands outside Goodison inscribed 'Footballer, Gentleman, Evertonian'. In 2002, at the National Football Museum Hall of Fame, Dixie became an inaugural inductee. In 2003 Littlewood's Football Pools sponsored the new Dixie Dean Award for Everton's Personality of the Year. Praise indeed coming from the family name most associated with Everton's neighbourly rivals, Liverpool FC!

Ken Dodd

'How Tickled I Am!
Everything's Plumptious and Tattifilarious!'

Yes, of course I remember Ken Dodd,' said the little old lady in the retirement home. 'He's that young whacker who comes round knocking on the door in Knotty Ash, selling household goods. I've bought mops and dishcloths and feather dusters from him. He still lives in that cottage in Thomas Lane.'

Her memories were accurate. After leaving the Holt High School for Boys at Childwall Fiveways, Kenneth Arthur Dodd hawked domestic items from door to door. His grandmother was a magistrate and his father was the local coal merchant, always good company and full of fun. His dad was also a talented musician and often went over to the Isle of Man to play both the saxophone and the clarinet in summer shows. Ken grew up with his brother and sister in Knotty Ash. Their childhood was happy and secure, their mother loving, supportive and very careful with the family finances. She too was musical and enjoyed playing the piano. Her warm-hearted nature helped to encourage a feeling of self-confidence in her children, frequently telling them, 'You can do anything you want to and you can be anything you want to be. As long as you try hard enough.'

Ken's parents fostered the young boy's imagination, regularly taking him to variety shows in the big Liverpool theatres of the time. The young lad always had creative ideas. He once painted his mum's draining board for her, using a nice thick coating of melted chocolate. Being too adventurous on his two-wheeler bike resulted in a nasty accident that redesigned his dental line-up for him. At the time it was unbearably painful but later in life it brought some toothsome rewards. Like his dad, Ken enjoyed hearing people laugh. When little schoolboy Ken sent off for a cheap mail-order manual on ventriloquism, his parents got him a ventriloquist's dummy for his birthday and Ken set about teaching himself the tricks of the trade. Very soon, as well as singing in the church choir, he progressed to entertaining at charity functions and performing in Scouts' gang shows, even earning a bob or two in the process.

Ken's comical creation of the all-singing, all-dancing Diddymen, living near the Jam Butty Mines of Knotty Ash, added fairytale fun to his act. In more classical vein, he played Malvolio, to great critical acclaim, in the 1972 production of *Twelfth Night* at the Liverpool Playhouse. So much so, that Kenneth Branagh introduced a specially surreal moment for him, as Yorick, in his film *Hamlet*. Normally, Yorrick is only referred to, not seen. But Branagh brought Hamlet's memories to life in the form of a flashback featuring Doddy.

In his long and enormously successful life, Ken has played nearly every venue in the British Isles. As well as clubs, theatres and variety halls, he has appeared at least twice at Liverpool's huge Royal Philharmonic Concert Hall, once at the age of twelve, with his comical dummy Charlie Brown and once, in more mature years, in 2004,

contributing to the series of illustrious Roscoe Memorial Lectures. These lectures all have the same theme – citizenship – but speakers are free to interpret the idea in their own way. It was fascinating to see the immaculately dressed Mr Dodd OBE at the lectern. He kept strictly to the subject. His words of wisdom included the comment 'We all try to be responsible citizens but nobody's perfect . . . (pause for effect) . . Except grandchildren!'

Ken's melodious light baritone voice is perfect for romantic ballads such as 'Love Is Like A Violin,' 'Happiness', 'Tears For Souvenirs' and 'So Deep Is The Night' which all feature strongly in his shows. From the early days of his career, Ken has always been willing to try something new and to give other struggling youngsters a chance. One young Scouser, too poor to own a piano, persuaded a friend to hire an old van, drive him up to Blackpool to study Ken's style, go round to the stage door and persuade Ken to listen to some tunes he had composed. They would meet at the mate's home and use his piano, supper being supplied by the pal's young wife. Ken readily agreed and a few days later the informal audition duly took place.

Of course, the characteristic for which Doddy is so famous is his rapid rendition of quickfire one-liners. Crazy, anarchic, surreal and irresistible, his wise-cracks constantly have his devoted fans in paroxysms of laughter. Many have been known to choose their holiday destinations according to where Doddy is appearing in summer season. He is also infamous for the length of his performances. He loves entertaining so much, he doesn't know when he's had enough. He warns his audiences that an evening with him is a challenge to the kidneys. No one ever complains. They are too weak with laughter. How they ever get home after their coaches have all turned back into pumpkins at midnight is a mystery. He loves a captive audience. Once, at the end of his act for the inmates of Dartmoor Prison, way out in the wilds of the Devonshire moors, he thanked them for being so appreciative. 'You've been so good,' he told them, 'I've organised a cross country run for everybody!'

His rise to stardom was the result of hard work and careful study. As he toured Britain, he noted the reactions to his gags in different regions. He tells people, 'You can tell a good joke in Glasgow but in Manchester there won't even be a titter. That's because they can't hear it from that distance.'

Although he has never married, Ken has had two long-standing romantic relationships. His first fiancée was Anita Boutin, a nurse who later became his secretary, helping him to correlate all his research on the mysteries of humour. Sadly, she died at an early age, leaving Ken heartbroken and determined to do everything in his power to raise funds for medical and other charities. He has been tireless in his support and appearances for good causes. Everyone knows that Ken's

29

beaming face at any event attracts hundreds of supporters and assures success. His present fiancée is long-term partner Anne Jones who has stood by him through thick and thin.

Always modest when not on stage (in fact it's impossible for him to blow his own trumpet), Ken lives a frugal life. Neither fast cars, swimming pools, nor mansions hold any interest for him. It is not so very long ago that he gave up sitting with all the other patients in the communal waiting room for Dr Jones and Dr Edwards, and visiting the local dentist in West Derby Village.

When a cloud appeared on his horizon in 1989, in the form of a trial for tax evasion, Ken spent five nail-biting weeks in court, answering charges of hoarding cash and notes in his cottage, rather than investing his fortune and declaring it to the Inland Revenue. Although he was finally acquitted by a local jury, he did have to pay crippling legal fees, as well as astronomical tax repayments and penalties. Many earnest theories have been propounded in the press and elsewhere as to Ken's psychological profile regarding money. One clue might date back to his mother's influence. She used to be the cash collector for the family coal delivery business, walking round on dark winter evenings with the payments in notes and coins jingling in her bag. Then, when Ken started earning, she guarded his money for him, storing it away in shoe-boxes rather than banking it.

Hard on the heels of the tax scandal, another black moment manifested itself in the form of a dangerous female stalker. Initially an ardent admirer, she developed a warped infatuation for Ken. After setting fire to his cottage, pushing a dead rat through his letter box and sending weird photographs of herself, she was arrested and taken to court. Following this, Ken's health needed time to recover but he soon bounced back, incorporating gags and references to his own legal proceedings into a new script. He began introducing himself as, 'Kenneth Arthur Dodd, singer, photographic playboy and failed accountant'. He then mentions the history of taxation. 'In previous centuries,' he says, 'income tax was only tuppence in the pound . . . I thought it still was!'

In 2004, Nottingham celebrated Ken's fifty years in show business at a sell-out performance to commemorate his first ever professional appearance at their Empire Theatre, in 1954. Long ago, Ken received the Freedom of the City of Liverpool. Referring to a crowded town-centre shopping precinct, Ken proudly boasts, 'Of course, you realise that I am now entitled to drive my flock of sheep down Bold Street! Tatty bye, everybody! Tatty bye!' And then breaks into a rousing rendition of 'Happiness'.

Despite undergoing surgery in 2008, Ken continued to attend numerous Capital of Culture events, appear at charity functions and support local hospitals and social concerns.

Ray Dunbobbin

Merseyside's Man of Many Talents

Always ready to see the funny side of life, Ray Dunbobbin had a fund of humorous experiences to share with others. Although he was an actor and writer, not a stand-up comedian, he often had after-dinner audiences rolling in the aisles without actually telling any jokes. A moment he frequently recalled with a smile was when, on location for a television programme, everything was organised and prepared for filming, actors in costume and positions, cameras all set to roll, when the director asked the sound technician if he was ready, 'No, no, no!' was the irritable reply. 'We can't start yet. One of the actors is breathing!'

Jokingly, Ray would say things that made people think twice. One of his favourites at Christmas time was, 'I've got more friends than I realised. I always get more cards than I receive.'

Ray was born in Ontario, Canada, but only because his Liverpudlian parents were living there at the time. When Ray was a year old, the family returned to Wavertree, Liverpool, and continued to live there. Ray's mother, Louise, had been a Salvation Army girl so Ray always had a soft spot for the down-to-earth practical help given by the 'Sally Army' to people in need and he was always ready to support their work. Sadly, Louise died very young. The shock had a traumatic effect on little Ray who, at the age of seven, was careless crossing a busy road. He was knocked

Ray Dunbobbin with Miss Liverpool, Maureen Martin.

down by a car. Among other injuries, both his legs were broken. He suffered life-long after-effects, including walking difficulties and an extended disruption to his education.

Long after the Second World War, as a young volunteer in the RAF, Ray signed the Official Secrets Act because of his work analysing aerial photographs of foreign landscapes, as well as deciphering messages in Morse code.

On returning to civvy street, Ray became a professional photographer and commercial artist, with an interest in music and theatre. He joined the Playgoers' Dramatic Society in Crown Street, Liverpool. Previous members had been the film star John Gregson and television's Leonard Rossiter, Rita Tushingham and Ken Jones. After one of the society's performances, the director, Mildred Spencer, came backstage and said to Ray, 'There is a talent scout from MGM in the audience and he wants to speak to you.' Ray laughed at the joke but Mildred wasn't joking. Ray was offered a tiny part in a John Gregson film being shot at Cammell Laird's shipyards at Birkenhead. He was thrilled to be picked up from home in a huge limousine, driven through the Mersey Tunnel and returned in the same manner at the end of filming. This taste of show business resulted in Ray turning professional and gaining parts in an abundance of films and television programmes from *Coronation Street* and *Emmerdale* to *Doctor Who*, *The Good Life*, *Last Of The Summer Wine*, *The Flaxton Boys* and *How We Used To Live*. In the latter, he played a greengrocer who had to shake hands with Liverpool actress Doreen Sloane. On camera, into her outstretched hand he slipped a huge, raw carrot. Her scream nearly deafened the sound technician! While appearing in *Porridge* as the batty Welshman, Evans, who ate shaving cream, boot polish, broken mirrors and razor blades, Ray became friendly with the wonderful young actor, Richard Beckinsale. Richard gave Ray and his wife complimentary tickets to see him in the West End farce, *I Love My Wife*. Soon afterwards, it was with great sadness that Ray learned that the charismatic Richard had died so tragically young at the age of thirty-one.

As well as acting, Ray had taken up writing for stage and screen. In 1972, the Liverpool Playhouse theatre mounted a three-week world premier of Ray's historical drama, *Black Spot On The Mersey*, based on the life and philanthropic work of Father James Nugent. It dealt with the disastrous aftermath of the 1840 Irish potato famine, causing death, disease, dire poverty and hundreds of orphans abandoned without food or shelter. Research involved detailed study of Father Nugent's own handwritten diaries kindly on loan from the Nugent Care Society, other archives and many interviews with knowledgeable clerics including Bishop Harris. Local actors were engaged for the production and many child actors from Liverpool drama schools had their first experience of professional work. The play increased awareness of Liverpool's history and made an enormous emotional impact on the audience.

Doreen Sloane, Phil Redmond, Jim Wiggins and Ray Dunbobbin.

Ray's research has benefited subsequent historians and writers. The BBC invited Ray to adapt the script for radio and it was produced by the young Alan Ayckbourn.

Ray also wrote scripts for *Z Cars*, *The Blazing Ocean* and the BBC *Suspense* series. His play *A Thing Like Death* was produced on Spanish television. His stage play, *Just Once Before You Go*, was produced at the Mountview Theatre, London.

BBC Radio Merseyside invited Ray to write a soap opera for them. Called *45 Derby Terrace*, it again employed only local actors. The *Liverpool Daily Post and Echo* liked the idea so much they asked Ray to adapt it for their newspaper and they serialised many episodes. At the same time, with a group of other Merseyside young entertainers, Ray was writing, producing and acting in a series of revues under the aegis of the English Speaking Union, whose chairman was Denis Rattle, father of Sir Simon Rattle. These musical and comedy shows were performed at the Liverpool University Theatre. All proceeds were donated to the Liverpool School of Tropical Medicine and to Mersey Kidney Research.

At the Playgoers' Club, Ray wrote a musical romance. All the parts were cast and in rehearsal, except for one character – an elderly French café owner. Among the members there was no one suitable. One evening, two young men, cousins, arrived, asked if they might join the company and perhaps take a part. Ray explained about the old character and auditioned them. He chose one of them, Brian Epstein, and asked the other to understudy. Brian adapted readily to the aging process required. The whole show proved a great success with excellent reviews in the *Daily Post and Echo*. Brian, of course, went on to have a somewhat different road to fame!

Some years later, when Carla Lane was looking for a 'father' for Lucien (Michael Angelis) and Carol (Elizabeth Estensen), in her hugely popular *Liver Birds*, Ray was cast in the part although he was only ten years older than Michael. 'In one Christmas scene,' Ray used to recall, 'I was driving a bus and paused at a make-believe stop in Paradise Street. A distinguished violinist from the Liverpool Phil was acting as a down-and-out busker, dirty, unshaven and wearing ragged mittens. A real drunk appeared, looked at the violinist's frozen fingers, pulled out a pair of fur-lined gloves, shoved them at the actor and slurred, ''Ere, you 'ave these, you poor ol' blighter. I've just nicked 'em from Lewis's. I'll go back for some more.' After recording all of Cyril Abraham's Liverpool shipping saga, *The Onedin Line*, as audio books, Phil Redmond's West Derby soap opera, *Brookside*, provided Ray with a long and fruitful run. Here, the good-natured widower Ralph Hardwick teamed up with the also widowed, but cantankerous, Harry Cross (Bill Dean) for many years of bickering yet humorous companionship, while each enjoyed a succession of lady-friends and eccentric adventures.

Actors become accustomed to being approached in public and asked for autographs. 'After I'd been in *Brookside* for about five years,' said Ray, 'I was in a restaurant in Church Stretton. A very attractive lady came up to our table, smiled warmly at me and said, "It is you, isn't it? I'd recognise you anywhere. You have made us so happy. It's been about five years now, hasn't it? I want to thank you on behalf of all my family. Oh, here's my husband. Darling, look who's here. It's that man who rescued our cat for us".'

Dr William Henry Duncan

The First Ever UK Medical Officer of Health

The Liverpool accent is claimed to be a mixture of Welsh, Irish and catarrh! This is due to three influences, Merseyside's proximity to North Wales, the great influx of Irish families after the Irish potato famine and the damp atmosphere of the North West coastal area.

But we must not forget the Merseyside Scots who also maintain a fine tradition in the city. There are Scottish dance societies, Hogmanay parties, Burns Nights and an extremely long list in the telephone directory of names beginning with Mc or Mac. The Liverpool Scottish Regiment has a history to be proud of and has strong connections with Liverpool College and with the heroic twins Noel and Christopher Chavasse.

Another of Liverpool's frequent claims is that we had the First Medical Officer of Health. Although Dr William Duncan was born at 23 Seel Street, Liverpool, he was of Scottish descent, as his surname suggests. He studied at Edinburgh University and qualified in Medical Jurisprudence, at that time a totally new subject. Until then, it was not taught anywhere else in the UK. After obtaining his degree, he loyally returned to Liverpool.

His early career involved the interesting contrast of one practice in Rodney Street, the 'Harley Street' of Liverpool and, at the same time, another in the Liverpool North Dispensary in Vauxhall Road. In those days this was one of the worst slum areas in the city, with appalling housing conditions, virtually no sanitation and overcrowding beyond belief.

William Duncan was nineteen years younger than Kitty Wilkinson (see p. 133). He was highly educated at one of the most prestigious seats of learning in the land. Kitty had no formal education at all but they both lived and worked during the same disgraceful period in Liverpool's history and they both had the same ideals and visionary concern for their contemporaries. William was totally dedicated to his work and always outspoken in condemnation of the city council's apathy concerning matters of hygiene and housing.

In 1832, as well as an influx of destitute Irish families, a cholera epidemic was steadily eating its way across Europe and Russia, arriving in Britain initially in Sunderland. At that time, there was still debate in the medical profession and confusion among the general public as to how this infection was spread. Many physicians thought it was a contagious disease, transmitted only by touch. Others were convinced that foul air, bad sanitation, infestation by cockroaches or vermin, dampness, malnutrition or even hysteria were the causes. Certainly all of these were rife among the downtrodden poor of the Vauxhall district. Miasma, from the Greek for pollution, was a word in common use at the time.

Dr Duncan, along with his colleague Dr David Baird, campaigned loud and long for slum clearance, re-housing and a radical approach to hygiene. It took strong words and tireless lobbying before any action was even planned by the town council. But, eventually, the crusade began to have some effect. The trouble was, knocking down old houses before building new ones only added to the hundreds of homeless. They simply crowded into other cellars and derelict buildings and things went from bad to worse. Starving, infected people now had anger and frustration to add to their woes. No wonder these sufferers regarded the practical and indefatigable Kitty Wilkinson as a saint, and had such lasting respect for Dr Duncan.

As well as treating his patients, William Duncan researched their living conditions and published this research in the *Liverpool Medical Gazette* in 1833. He made it clear that deaths from the disease were much more frequent among those in the overcrowded cellars than among families living in 'normal' households.

His views and criticism made him extremely unpopular among the hierarchy. They didn't want their dirty linen washed in public, neither literally nor metaphorically. Because he exposed a certain patent medicine as 'quackery' and deemed it useless in the treatment of cholera and refused to prescribe it, the *Liverpool Mercury* printed an emotive piece calling him a murderer. But he persevered with his campaigning and eventually forced through the Liverpool Sanitary Act of 1846.

The bureaucrats eventually decided to create a post known as Medical Officer of Health. At least they had the sense to appoint the most suitable applicant for the task! A long, hard struggle awaited him, especially as typhus now raged in the Vauxhall and Scotland Road areas. Dr Duncan joined other critics of the 'Black Spot on the Mersey', as Liverpool was known, condemning his home town as 'the unhealthiest place in England.'

It took many years of single-minded dedication before the First Medical Officer of Health and his colleague, the first Borough Engineer, James Newland, began to see any progress. But it is to him and his successors that Liverpool owes its greatly improved health services and its continuing construction work on hospitals, medical centres and university research departments.

The teaching block in the Royal Liverpool University Hospital is now named the Duncan Building in his honour and, since the pub in Seel Street has been renamed the Blue Angel, another pub in St John's Lane now proudly bears his name and houses replicas of two portraits of the worthy physician, one as a young man and one as the mature and respected benefactor that he was.

Ronnie Finn 1930–2004
The Doctor who Saved Millions of Babies' Lives

'The Department of Medicine at Liverpool University is the source of one of the twentieth-century's greatest medical research advances. To date, millions of human deaths and great suffering have been averted by the brilliant work of Ronnie Finn and his department chief, Sir Cyril Clarke, by the prevention of Rhesus haemolytic disease of the newborn for which they were given the Lasker Award, known as the American Nobel Prize.'

From *The Double Helix*, David Zimmerman, James D. Watson

Ronald Finn was born in Liverpool and devoted his life's work to the people of Merseyside. Ultimately, his brilliant intuition, his research and his findings have benefited countless mothers and babies throughout the world. In order to qualify as a doctor, Ronnie studied diligently during his schooldays and progressed, with the aid of City and State Scholarships, to graduate from Liverpool University in 1954 with MB ChB, adding Membership of the Royal College of Physicians in 1958, a Doctorate of Medicine in 1961, Fellowship of the Royal College of Physicians in 1972 and an Honorary FRCPCH in 1996. Prior to his undergraduate days, he had served as a private in the Royal Army Medical Corps.

His leisure time interests and hobbies were varied. He never missed a Saturday afternoon home match at St Helens Rugby Club, he loved reading mysteries and enjoyed foreign travel. He was also fascinated by the tombs in the Valley of the Kings in Egypt.

Early in his career he studied with Sir Cyril Clarke and later became his house physician and registrar. On a visit to London, Ronnie met and fell in love at first sight with Joan. Their happy marriage lasted until his death in 2004. They had two children and two grandchildren of whom he was justly proud. Recently, his widow wrote: 'There is so much to say about Ronnie, it is difficult to know where to begin. He was a great humanist; adored by his patients and pupils. Not only was he the doctors' doctor but he was the consultants' consultant. The families of his colleagues relied upon his diagnosis and treatment and greatly respected his judgment. Even now, years after his death, people tell me how much they miss him.'

Until Ronnie's research, many young parents through the ages were at a loss to understand how and why it was possible for them to have a healthy first baby but their second and subsequent babies were either still-born, born with jaundice, with severe anaemia or were grossly swollen at birth. With any of these conditions the babies were likely to die within a few days of delivery. Throughout the preceding centuries, no one had realised that the lottery of who married who and the combination of their genetic blood groups held the key to the mystery of these deaths. Ronnie worked on the principle that during labour a small number of the

baby's red cells are now known to be squeezed back into the mother's circulation via the placenta. If the baby contained the Rhesus positive gene but the mother was Rhesus negative, her blood could react against the invading blood cells from her baby, thus affecting any later Rhesus positive pregnancy.

However, Haemolytic Disease in the newborn occurred only in a proportion of such cases. Why was this? After painstaking and prolonged study of a large number of Merseyside pregnancies, Ronnie concluded that the relevant factor was the compatibility or incompatibility of the baby's ABO blood group, as used in blood transfusions, with the mother's ABO blood group. If they were compatible, the baby's red cells squeezed into the maternal circulation would survive and their Rhesus content would evoke a maternal antibody response. This would endanger any subsequent Rhesus positive pregnancy. If the baby's and mother's blood were ABO incompatible, any of the baby's red cells entering the maternal circulation would be rapidly destroyed before they had the opportunity of evoking Rhesus antibodies. In that case, the subsequent Rhesus positive pregnancies would not be affected. Ronnie realised that an injection of the antibody against the Rhesus factor into the mother soon after labour, might afford protection by quickly destroying any of the baby's red cells that had managed to enter the maternal circulation, before these cells had an opportunity of immunising the mother against any future Rhesus encounter. The theory proved to be correct. The treatment worked perfectly. Second and subsequent babies of treated Rhesus negative mothers remained healthy. The treatment was quickly adopted worldwide. Millions of babies' lives have thus been saved and the terrible grief of young parents losing a much longed-for second child has been averted. The treatment now bears the name of 'The Liverpool Shot.'

Ronnie, Sir Cyril and a group of American researchers who were working on the same problem were presented with the Lasker Award, the American equivalent of the Nobel Prize. Not content with this most satisfying outcome of his research, Ronnie extended his studies into other aspects of immunology, with special interest in the effect of the environment on human health. At that time, few physicians concerned themselves with environmental reactions, so Dr Finn founded the British Society for Allergy and Environmental Medicine. He felt sure that, apart from inherited tendencies, a person's environment, diet and lifestyle greatly influences their well-being and life span. In recent decades, these far-seeing ideas have been acknowledged as fundamental truths and have been universally adopted. He also took a particular interest in food intolerances, hay fever, asthma, high blood pressure, heart attacks and Crohn's disease.

After his retirement, he was awarded a personal Chair of Medicine by Liverpool University. Professor Finn's popular lectures and writing helped to reach a wide audience for his findings and achievements. When genetically modified foods appeared, Professor Finn was requested to go to the House of Lords to speak on behalf of those who urged caution.

In his leisure time, after two visits to Egypt, Professor Finn set himself the task of solving the riddle of the curse of early death of the archaeologists who opened Tutankhamun's tomb. He proposed a practical, though yet unproven, medical solution to the uncanny events and held audiences enthralled with his gift as a natural raconteur. To hear Professor Finn speak at any meeting, medical or social, was always a great pleasure for his audiences. His clarity of diction was matched by the warm tone of his voice, his enthusiasm for his subject and the breadth of his knowledge.

Anthony & Eric George and Primrose Agbamu (née Leigh)

Members of the Oldest Known Liverpool Family

In 1207, King John bestowed a charter upon Liverpool, granting it the right to be known as a city. In 2007, the Liverpool Culture Company decided to commemorate the city's 800th birthday. Celebrations were many and varied, one of the most intriguing being a search for the Liverpool family able to trace its ancestry further back into the past than any other family.

At the request of his daughters, Eric George had already undertaken considerable research into his own family genealogy. What he discovered was amazing. With the aid of the internet and by scrutinising old documents in churches and parish registers, he was able to bring to light family surnames, births, marriages and deaths dating right back to 1543 during the reign of Henry VIII. Unbeknown to Eric and Anthony, they had a cousin, Primrose, who had been conducting her own survey. She too was unaware that she had relatives nearby. Of all the families who entered the competition, brothers Eric and Anthony and by coincidence, Primrose, had the best evidence to prove their claims. However, Primrose and Eric no longer

Anthony and Pauline George, members of Liverpool's most historic family.

live in Liverpool but, fortunately, Anthony still lives within the boundaries of the city. So it was left to him to claim the prize. He and his wife Pauline have been fêted, photographed and interviewed. They have attended all sorts of civic functions. They rode with the Lord Mayor at the head of the Lord Mayor's Procession and mixed with local celebrities at parties and charity events. They have thoroughly enjoyed the honour, not to mention meeting Primrose for the first time and discovering yet another branch of their family tree. In their early days, both Eric and Anthony attended Sylvester Infants and Junior School in Huyton. Then

Eric, Alan and Anthony (in pram) with their parents.

Eric went to Wade Deacon Grammar in Widnes and followed that by becoming a student at Byrom Street Technical College in Liverpool. Anthony went to Hey County Secondary in Huyton and then studied at St Helens Technical College. Altogether, their education spanned the years between 1939 and 1962.

'Before researching our heritage, our present-day claims to fame were these', says Anthony. 'We lived in the same road as Stuart Sutcliffe, known as the fifth Beatle, who sadly died before the group reached its greatest fame. Also, I attended college with Alec Murphy, of St Helens Rugby and Great Britain fame. Now we and Primrose all feel quite famous ourselves since proving we are the most historic family in Liverpool.'

The earliest proof of the family's heritage is dated 1543, when a certain Thomas Wodley was born in Childwall. His daughter Katherine married a Johannes Grace and continued to live in Childwall. They were succeeded by their son and grandson, Thomas Grace and Henry Grace. Then came an Isaac Grace born in Allerton and another Thomas Grace in Wavertree. The next Thomas Grace was born in Speke, in 1695. He rented Speke Hall for a number of years.

The members of the competition's judging panel were particularly interested to learn of this as, until the proof of the Grace family lineage was unearthed, there had been a gap in the city records. No one had previously been able to verify what had happened in Speke Hall during that period. Anecdotal evidence now implies that this generation of the Grace family were farmers and were accused of using the Great Parlour as a milking shed for their dairy herd. Primrose takes a sceptical attitude to that, although she does admit, 'The Great Parlour would have been ideal for this, as it had a door leading straight out into the grounds. The Grace family was also accused of using the fireplaces for cooking. Didn't everyone, at that time? After all, there were twenty hearths in the place. Some mention was also made of them using tapestries for horse blankets. Typical Liverpudlian "Red Rum" treatment! Only the best for our livestock! The youngsters of that era were just like teenagers today. They carved their names on the rafters. These beams have since been replaced. What vandalism!' she exclaims. 'Destroying historic relics! Just think of how valuable they might have become!' Certainly the names would have provided a record as to who exactly was living on the hall during the mystery years. The actual owners of the hall were the Norris family. In 1731, the property passed to a Mary Norris. When she married Lord Sidney Beauclerk, grandson of Nell Gwynne, she became a 'Lady' and moved to London. The hall was then sold to the Watts family and further generations of the Grace family left Speke and became flour dealers in Toxteth Park.

Robert Grace (born in 1770) married a French girl, Clotilde Vallet, whose father, Mathieu Vallet, had brought the process of bleaching to Britain. He had set up a bleach works near the salt works in Garston. It is claimed that back in France he had taken King Louis XVI and Marie Antoinette up in a hot air balloon in 1785. Subsequent members of the Grace family lived in the moated mansion known as Old Hutte in the Speke area. Because families were so large in times gone by, there were always enough sons to carry the same surname through the generations but in 1877, a change of name appears. Elizabeth Grace married Joseph Leigh and it is from this distaff line that Primrose Agbamu (née Leigh) is descended. Eric and Anthony George's grandmother also had the surname Leigh. Sadly, she died of tuberculosis in the Whiston Workhouse Infirmary in 1913, when her daughter Gladys, was only three years old. When Gladys grew up, she married Walter George and they became the parents of the present generation, Eric, Anthony and their late brother Alan, the winners of the competition.

In previous centuries, the Speke Hall Estate extended much further than the present grounds. There was once woodland where the runway of the John Lennon Airport now stretches. Another part of the parkland and the site of Old Hutte is now buried beneath the Jaguar car factory. As the Childe of Hale was born in 1578, it is more than likely that the ancestors of Eric, Anthony and Primrose would have known about and even seen the giant who became for a while the body guard at Speke Hall.

'There used to be a wood on the Speke Hall Estate, called Grace's Wood,' explains Primrose, 'right under where the John Lennon Airport runway is now! I was considering getting a working party together to dig up the runway and transplant a wood. We could have demolished the Jaguar factory while we were at it. But I discovered that the descendants of another of Henry's sons, Thomas, planted a Grace's Wood in Knowsley, Merseyside, so I'll make do with that until they start building homes there, the same as everywhere else in the vicinity.'

Steven Gerrard

Liverpool Football Club's Perfection on Legs

Were it not for one tiny blip when Steven Gerrard, in a moment of madness, allowed himself to consider, albeit briefly, a tempting offer from Chelsea, the young Liverpool player would probably be considered flawless by his thousands of devoted fans. Steven's childhood days were spent in Huyton and Whiston and, apart from his family, his greatest love is Liverpool Football Club. His dedication to the game is unquestionable and his natural talent makes his every move seem effortless. His outstanding skills were apparent from a very early age. He was spotted at eight years of age and later coached by Steve Heighway. Noted for his adaptability and far-reaching shots, he is equally at home in various midfield positions. In 1998, he was the PFA Young Player of the Year. Having graduated with honours from the youth team, his reputation as one of the best midfielders in Europe spread far and wide. Thanks to Kevin Keegan, Steven made his England debut in 2000 and, in 2001, he helped his country to a 5–1 victory over Germany with his first international goal.

Everyone knows that in any fast-moving sport there are bound to be injuries but Steven has overcome his teenage 'growing pains', owing probably to hormonal changes associated with his adolescent height increase. He tackles all problems with a calm determination. Although he has sometimes been required to play in uncharacteristic positions, his speed and accuracy have often transformed defence into attack, bewildering the opposition and putting the ball in unbelievably inch-perfect locations. He can rival David Beckham for the ease with which he can bend a right-wing cross and his running speed could, in other circumstances, rival Red Rum. He frequently outwits the most daunting of would-be markers with his expressive body language and his audacious evasions. He has been voted Player of the Year, twice Premier League Most Valuable Player of the Year and UEFA Most Valuable Player of the Year.

In the 2001 season, against Manchester United, Steven's dream goal was voted the best ever in a Premiership match. His amazing passes are a gift to his team mates. In particular, the late decider at Old Trafford in 2002 owed much to Gerrard's archer-like dispatch to Danny Murphy. Injury kept him away from the 2002 World Cup but by 2003 he was captain of the Reds and in 2004 he skippered his country against Sweden. In 2005, Steven played right-back in the Champions League Final and in 2006 his two goals in the FA Cup Final against West Ham turned the game around. Steven's investiture with the MBE at Buckingham Palace was filmed and shown on television in December 2007. In the same month, his neat contribution helped his team on the amazing 8–0 score against Besiktas.

But December 2007 was full of mixed blessings. While Steven was still elated at his contributing goal in the decisive away triumph over Marseille, he received news that, at home, his wife had been terrified by masked raiders who plundered the

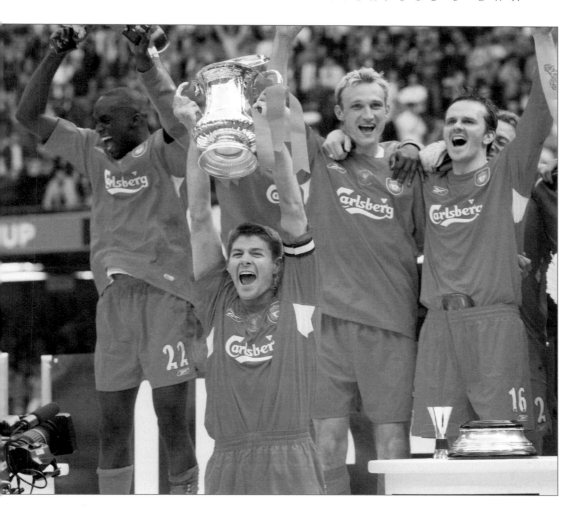

house and got away with thousands of pounds worth of jewellery. Thankfully, their two daughters slept safely through it all and Alex herself was not physically harmed.

As compliments go, it would be hard to beat this: 'Gerrard is the most influential player in England, bar none. Everywhere the ball is, he is there.' Unbelievably, this generous tribute comes from no one associated with Anfield, nor the training ground at Melwood, but from a grudgingly honest Sir Alex Ferguson, manager of rivals Manchester United.

William Gladstone 1809–96

Four Times Prime Minister of Great Britain

There are many portraits of William Gladstone, mainly as an elder statesman. Most depict a stern and inflexible-looking Victorian patriarch. The eyes are almost expressionless and the mouth is clamped shut with the corners turned down, as if in disapproval. One photograph shows him with bushy, shoulder-length white hair and the characteristic turned-down lips. Of course, by this time in his life, he had the weight of great responsibility upon his shoulders. By contrast, in private, he was warm-hearted, loving, jovial and very popular with young children.

William Ewart Gladstone was born at 62 Rodney Street, known as the Harley Street of Liverpool because of the many medical specialists with consulting rooms there. His date of birth puts him as a contemporary of both Abraham Lincoln and Charles Darwin. William's father was Sir John Gladstone, a wealthy and highly successful merchant. Both Sir John and his second wife, Anne, were of Scottish descent and William was the fifth of their six children. Although Sir John had a very affectionate and genial nature, they followed a strict, evangelical regime. When the family moved from Rodney Street to a large new house near the mouth of the River Mersey, William's first school was situated in a rectory called Seaforth Vicarage. Six years later, he became a boarder at Eton College near Windsor Castle. At Christ Church College, Oxford, he gained a double first in Classics and Mathematics. He became President of the Oxford Union Debating Society and was admired for his eloquence and the breadth of his knowledge. At university, he was a Tory, opposed to Whig ideas of reform. He enjoyed both Eton and Oxford immensely and made many lasting friendships.

William's personality was one of great complexity, with puzzling and contradictory characteristics. As a young man, he was energetic and at times very impetuous. Deeply held religious convictions and an iron will usually helped him to overcome any rash behaviour, but not always. He was happy and earnest with huge mental and physical prowess but he often doubted himself and lacked confidence. He had an athletic build, slim with fine muscular shoulders, yet he took no exercise nor interest in sport of any kind. In his early days he was extremely handsome with attractive eyes, good bone structure and dark wavy hair; nevertheless, his first attempts at courting young ladies were met with total indifference and immediate refusal. He fell in love at first sight on a regular basis and proposed to at least two very young women in quick succession, sending long and complicated letters to their respective parents, importuning them to give consent to what they considered entirely unsuitable matches. In both cases, the young ladies and their families felt that William was too straight-laced and domineering in his outlook on life. The girls could see no reason to give up their social activities, sporting hobbies and dancing to marry someone they hardly knew. At different times, both sets of parents had to tell him quite bluntly that all correspondence must cease.

By contrast, William could immerse himself in his studies to the exclusion of all else. He was widely read in religious, philosophical and classical Greek literature. In order to acquaint himself with the works of German theologians, he learned German in an amazingly short time – he was already proficient in French and Italian. He became friendly with both Tennyson and Wordsworth but couldn't understand why Wordsworth wanted enfranchisement for country districts. As was the fashion of the time, William and one of his elder brothers, Lieutenant John Gladstone RN, went on the Grand Tour of Europe, the equivalent of today's gap year.

One of William's friends from his days at Eton, Lord Lincoln, persuaded his father, the Duke of Newcastle, to offer one of the Parliamentary seats under his control to William. Gladstone had thought of entering the Church but eventually agreed to stand for election. Strangely, his religious principles upheld the practice of flogging for certain crimes. When he was voted into office in 1833, he used his maiden speech to defend his father against accusations of ill-treatment of slaves on his plantation in the West Indies. Sir John, like his son, was also a man of incomprehensible inconsistencies. At home, a loving husband and father, to whom all his family were devoted; with colleagues genial and generous; by religion, a devout Christian; in his professional life, as with many other merchants, ship-owners and mill-owners of the time, he could see no harm in using slave labour to line his own pockets. William acknowledged that slavery was iniquitous. It 'unquestionably began in crime, in atrocious crime.' But William denied any cruelty on his father's land. In future arguments, Gladstone agreed that he was in favour of gradual steps towards emancipation, but he thought that immediate abolition would be of no use to slaves. Instead, he proposed a two-year apprenticeship period. In another speech he said, 'I cannot forget that English factory children are permitted to grow up in almost as great ignorance and deadness of heart as the West Indian Negroes.' He reminded the electors that four-fifths of all the goods that they themselves consumed were 'the product of slave labour in Lancashire and of a system even more injurious than that enforced in the West Indies.'

His rise in Parliament was swift. In December 1834, Sir Robert Peel appointed him Junior Lord of the Treasury and in January 1835 he became Under Secretary of State for the colonies.

Although unlucky in love at an earlier age, Gladstone eventually found the perfect soulmate. Catherine Glynne, sister of William's school friend, Sir Stephen Glynne, returned William's affection without hesitation. They married in 1839 and remained devoted to each other for life, bringing up a family of eight children and taking great delight in their grandchildren. When Gladstone began his crusade to save fallen women and persuade them to take up preferable occupations, Catherine gave him her wholehearted support and even accompanied him on many occasions on his walks, through the darkened streets where prostitutes plied there trade. She was utterly devout in her religious beliefs, had a lively sense of humour and took William's criticism of her artistically untidy household light-heartedly. With such a large family, neatness was rather difficult, even when they lived in her ancestral home at Hawarden Castle.

Sir Robert Peel appointed Gladstone to posts of Vice-President, then President of the Board of Trade in 1841 and 1843 respectively. In 1852 he was appointed Chancellor of the Exchequer. He had hoped to reduce income tax but actually needed to increase it from seven pence to ten pence ha'penny in the pound, in anticipation of government expenditure. But by 1860 he was able to introduce popular policies which reduced the cost of living. By stages, he managed to decrease income tax to four pence in the pound. He established the Post Office Savings Bank to enable low-income families some means of simple savings. For the Lancashire cotton workers thrown out of work owing to the blockade of Confederate ports in the USA, preventing the export of cotton, Catherine and William joined forces to provide work on their private estate at Hawarden.

As he matured, Gladstone's attitudes mellowed. He developed more humanitarian attitudes and joined the Liberal Party, but he was still unpopular in certain high places. Queen Victoria never took to him. She complained that even in private he addressed her 'like a public meeting'. She preferred the charming manners and elegant attire of Benjamin Disraeli. Needless to say, there was always hostility between Gladstone and Disraeli as they vied for the hearts and minds of the electorate.

By 1864, Gladstone realised that the constitution should be more flexible and he put forward the idea that every man of sound mind, however humble, should have the vote. In order to win this right, he expected them to show evidence of genuine understanding of political issues. There was, of course, no question of women having the vote, however high their status or intellectual capacity. It was to be New Zealand which became the first country to give votes to women.

In 1868, after holding a number of cabinet posts of the utmost importance, Gladstone became Prime Minister. During the next two decades, his attitudes became still more enlightened. Under his influence, life in Britain began to open up like a bud in the spring sunshine. He proposed to reduce public expenditure, therefore requiring less taxation and allowing individuals to choose for themselves how they spent their disposable incomes. Unnecessarily restrictive laws were reformed, allowing opportunities for people to climb out of their social class by personal effort. Flogging, which he had once condoned, was now forbidden in the services in peacetime. He was always in favour of Home Rule for Ireland and he forced through the Irish Land Act to shackle the powers of unscrupulous landlords.

During every phase of his political career, Gladstone confided in his wife. He had absolute faith in her integrity and intelligence and she was his ever-constant support in all matters both political and personal.

Disraeli became Prime Minister in 1874, after Gladstone and the Liberals were heavily defeated in a general election. A reversal of fortunes brought Gladstone back into power six years later. For two years, he acted as both Prime Minister and Chancellor of the Exchequer. But disaster struck when he hesitated instead of acting promptly to save General Gordon, besieged at Khartoum in Sudan. In spite of his campaigning for ethical foreign policies, this procrastination led to General Gordon's death and the massacre of the British forces. Overnight Gladstone's nickname changed from 'Grand Old Man', to 'Gordon's Own Murderer'. Resignation was the only option for him and he declined Queen Victoria's offer of an earldom.

In 1886, Gladstone became Prime Minister again, also taking on the responsibility of Lord Privy Seal. This was a short-lived term, lasting less than a year and he did not return to power until 1892, at the age of nearly eighty-three, still hoping for Ireland's independence. It was his domestic policies that made him popular. He introduced secret ballots, cheaper transport and communications, spent his own money opening homes for destitute women and put ecological office procedures into practice to cut down on waste and expense.

At the age of eighty-five, Gladstone bequeathed £40,000 as well as £32,000-worth of his own books to found the only residential library in Britain. It is known as St Deiniol's Library. True to his reputation for enormous stamina and energy, he would only allow one daughter and one servant to help transfer the books by wheelbarrow a quarter-of-a-mile to their new location.

The beautiful library in Church Lane, Hawarden, Flintshire, is still thriving and in constant use today. In keeping with modern technology, electronic records and other facilities are being introduced, a fitting memorial to the man whose aims were to bring enlightenment and educational opportunities to every sector of the community.

John Goldsmith
Hitler's Gift to Merseyside Medical Improvements

By 1979, the workforce and management at the Ford Motor Company, Halewood, had raised over £190,000 to donate to various local charities, not yet selected. When Dr John Goldsmith heard of this, knowing that his own Kidney Unit at Sefton General Hospital, was in danger of closure for economic reasons, he decided to make a plea for some of these funds. In the open air, standing on a little rise within the factory grounds (known as Pork Chop Hill), he addressed a huge gathering during the workmen's lunch hour. He described a revolutionary new invention, the brainchild of his American colleague Dr Kolff. It was a machine which could act as an artificial kidney. Never before had patients with kidney disease had any real hope of relief or cure. But this dialysis machine could perform the blood-cleansing process normally carried out by healthy kidneys. As Dr Goldsmith spoke to the crowd, it began to rain heavily. Such was the interest and understanding he created in this medical miracle, nobody moved indoors. Instead, the staff voted to donate the full amount to Dr Goldsmith's charity, Mersey Kidney Research, which has since helped thousands of patients with hitherto fatal kidney failure to survive and, with the aid of transplantation, to lead near-normal lives.

The precursor to this far-reaching benefit to the health of the North-West began in the years immediately before the Second World War. In Dusseldorf, Germany, John's father, a musically talented businessman who longed to become a professional cellist, died in his early fifties. While John was still a very young child, his mother, a dental surgeon, remarried. Her second husband, a handsome, esteemed and successful Jewish dentist had strong anti-Nazi views. In 1933 a rival and much less popular dentist, jealous, embittered and a Nazi enthusiast, with some accomplices kidnapped, tortured and murdered John's stepfather. They shot him, weighted his body down with a heavy printing press, then threw it into a reservoir. The body eventually became separated from its restraints, rose to the surface and the crime was discovered. Because of the murderers' influential political positions, no charges were brought against them until many years later after Germany's defeat.

John's shocked mother, realising Germany was no longer a safe place to bring up her only child, travelled to Holland where one of her brothers lived. John stayed for four years and his early schooling was entirely in Dutch. At this time, the little boy's tonsils and adenoids became infected. John still remembers the shock of the operation. 'I was lifted onto a huge male nurse's knee,' he says. 'He gripped both my legs between his. He locked both my arms behind my back with one hand and used the other to push back my head and force open my mouth. Then without any form of anaesthetic, the surgeon tore away my tonsils and adenoids. The pain and shock were so great that I was completely traumatised. I was beyond crying. I

Dr John Goldsmith (far right) with nurses, patients, doctors and *Brookside* actors at the Royal Liverpool University Hospital.

couldn't move nor utter any kind of sound at all. Much later, back at home, I cried incessantly for hours and hours.'

John's mother was not permitted to work as a dentist in Holland so she moved to Belgium and found a position as a demonstrator in the University Dental Hospital in Brussels. She tried to persuade her five brothers and sisters to leave Europe with their families. Only two did. The rest, along with their own children, perished in Hitler's gas chambers. John's widowed grandmother died alone and in hiding in Holland.

Eventually arriving in Britain in 1937, John's mother was welcomed as the highly qualified dentist she was. With the help of friends, she settled in Cambridge, numbering many brilliant and famous academics among her patients. John attended the Leys, a Methodist school, as a day boy although most pupils were boarders. He gradually learned perfect English, formed friendships which continue to this day, became an enthusiastic member of the school choir and made excellent progress with his studies. 'I was very happy at the Leys,' says John. 'Staff and fellow pupils were so kind and helpful and I really enjoyed my lessons. I soon felt like a genuine English schoolboy and knew I wanted to become part of English life.'

But another shock was in store for him. 'On my sixteenth birthday, I was sitting near a classroom window, just finishing an English essay, when I noticed a policeman striding across the quad to the headmaster's office. Although I knew I had done nothing wrong, I realised what was about to happen, as another pupil who was German by birth had been taken away and interned on *his* sixteenth birthday. Sure enough, I was escorted home, told to pack a few things and became an "enemy alien" simply by reaching the age of sixteen. The same misjudgement had been made during the First World War. People fleeing from persecution were mistaken for the persecutors and treated as potential criminals.' John's mother was allowed to stay because she was a woman and was needed to replace dentists who had enlisted in the forces.

Along with some of the most brilliant foreign academics at Cambridge, John was taken to Bury St Edmunds, then to Huyton, where local people misunderstood the situation and harassed them, thinking these refugees were actually the Nazis from whom they had escaped. The next internment camp was on the Isle of Man. Then came deportation in convoy to Canada where the weather became wintry. Instead of school subjects, John found himself used as a lumberjack, cutting down pines. His education was totally neglected. After nine months, the authorities realised their misjudgement and gave the young internees the option of being released in Canada or returning to Britain. As an only child with a twice-widowed mother at home, John's choice was obvious.

He was able to catch up at school and later qualified as a doctor at Guy's Hospital. Shortly afterwards, he gained the Membership of the Royal College of Physicians, a highly valued specialist qualification. Later, serving in the British Army, then working in America for eighteen months and eventually specialising in kidney disease, he was delighted to work for many years with a team of dedicated colleagues in Sefton General and later at the Royal Liverpool University Hospital. They all became close personal friends, especially physicians Dr Ronnie Finn, Dr Rasheed Ahmad, Dr Rana Rustom and surgeon Mr Norman Gibbon.

As well as his own ward rounds and clinical work as a consultant kidney specialist and founder member of Mersey Kidney Research, Dr Goldsmith took on the post of manager of the Royal Hospital with the specific aim of increasing efficiency and hygienic conditions. After semi-retirement at the age of sixty-five, he frequently travelled to North Wales to take clinics there. He now has a growing family of eleven grandsons and two granddaughters. 'Enough for a football team and two cheer-leaders,' he jokes. To mark his forty years on the Kidney Research committee, Anne Lloyd, MKR's events secretary and her husband Keith Aston of the Chester branch of the charity, arranged a special 'This Is Your Life' party for John, with tributes from grateful past patients, many colleagues, family and friends from his twenty-four years in the Liverpool Philharmonic Choir.

In spite of everything that has happened to him, including still grieving for the early loss of his daughter Caroline, John considers himself to be basically fortunate and is always looking for ways to give something back to the country that made such a welcome difference to his own life. Kidney Research is only one of many charities that he supports and, through everything, he has retained a positive attitude and sense of humour. At a dinner to honour his medical contributions to the well-being of Merseyside, he said, 'Fortunately, my "retro-spectoscope" has rose-tinted lenses!'

Among his many humorous experiences, he tells of one incident not related to work. 'Opposite our house,' he says, 'there was a petrol station and garage. Because of unpaid VAT, the business was closed down overnight. But the burglar alarm wasn't disconnected. One weekend, high winds activated it and the noise continued night and day. We tried to call the police but they said they could do nothing. All the neighbours were at their wits' end. No sleep. No peace at all. My next-door neighbour, a judge, suggested we should try to disconnect it ourselves. We put up a high ladder and tried. A screwdriver wouldn't work so we were just about to use a hammer when the police arrived. There was the usual "'Ello, 'ello, 'ello. What d'you think you are doing? And who'd you think you are?" "Well", said my neighbour, "He's a consultant doctor and I'm a county judge." "And I'm Micky Mouse!" said the constable. "Unless you desist forthwith, I shall have to arrest you. Now clear off or I'll have you for breaking and entering!"'

Reginald Carey Harrison 1908–90

Sir Rex Harrison – 'Sexy Rexy'

'He was so charming, warm, witty and so caring and sympathetic.' 'He was the rudest man on earth, fussy, self-centred, cold, calculating and with a foul temper.' 'He was so confident. He could glide through any situation without the flicker of an eyelid.' 'He was a bundle of nerves, suffered the most appalling stage-fright and had absolutely no confidence in himself.'

Who are these four very different people? They are all Rex Harrison, the cultured, debonair Hollywood film star, born in Huyton. He was such a complex bundle of contrasts, no two people had the same opinion of him, least of all any of his six wives.

It is interesting to note that the first Tony award won by Rex Harrison, for Best Actor in a Broadway production, was for his interpretation of King Henry VIII, who also had six wives and was ruthlessly cruel. Rex never had anyone beheaded but two of the women in his life did commit suicide and another died while married to him.

Reginald Carey Harrison (his given name) was born in 1908, in Huyton, just outside Liverpool city boundaries. Reginald was a sickly child, often confined to bed, his doting mother waiting on him hand and foot. His slightest wish was instantly catered for. This may well have been the root cause of his life-long tendency to finicky tastes and the habit of constantly changing his mind about his choice of menu or drinks.

The Huyton area near Roby Road, inhabited by the Harrison family was, at that time, still rural, with a few large and elegant dwellings. About 2 miles away, Reginald's grandfather's imposing residence, known as Belle Vale, was surrounded by private parkland. At a later date, this was demolished and today there is a modern housing estate and shopping precinct, also called Belle Vale, on that site. Reginald's first school was Huyton College For Girls. Little boys from genteel families were accepted into the kindergarten at that time. At the age of seven, Reginald suffered a severe attack of measles, causing him to lose the sight in one eye. Because of his diminished eyesight, Reginald had difficulty in seeing the blackboard properly and he was usually bottom of his class.

When the family moved back to Liverpool, after a spell in Sheffield, they lived much closer to the city centre, in a large Victorian terraced house, 10 Lancaster Avenue. Family trips to the theatre were frequent. At his first pantomime, Reginald was so entranced, he immediately decided that he would like to act. At home, he made his parents sit and watch him take elaborate bows between their dining room curtains, even though he hadn't bothered to earn any applause by singing, dancing or reciting. At eleven, Reginald enrolled at Liverpool College. Again he did not shine academically but he did join the drama group and the Officers' Training Corps. When he began Latin lessons, Reginald decided that he had had enough of

his given name. He thought 'Rex', meaning king, suited him better. In his career he played at least two world-famous kings, Henry VIII and the King of Siam, as well as the Emperor Julius Caesar, and a professor, a doctor and many aristocrats. His haughty bearing and somewhat superior attitude naturally suited these roles.

In spite of his early ambitions, Rex never had any formal drama training. On leaving school, he became an assistant stage manager at the Liverpool Playhouse, a lowly position actually meaning student and general dogsbody. The Liverpool Repertory Company had an extremely high reputation and was the alma mater of many distinguished stars but Rex made little impression and was actually advised to drop acting as a profession.

He next tried a touring company. For three years he travelled the country, learning his lines on train journeys, staying in cheap lodgings and trying to look elegant on what amounted to slave wages. Because of his one defective eye, he wore a monocle, which helped to create the illusion of learned refinement. Every week, his mother dutifully sent him a loving letter with a 10s note in it.

In 1934 he met and married Colette Thomas and they had a son named Noel. Even when married, however, Rex had a fondness for the ladies and the marriage struggled to last eight years.

When the Second World War broke out, Rex knew that his visual problems would debar him from active service, but he was keen to make himself available to help in any way possible. In the meantime he continued in the theatre. Unfortunately, the official blackout regulations, together with restricted public transport after dark, made evening performances impracticable. Instead, theatres mounted morning and matinée shows. Actors then spent most evenings in their hotel bars, drinking, talking and flirting. A young German actress, Maria Lilli Peiser, fled to Britain, via France, to escape the growing persecution in her homeland. She adopted the name Lili Palmer and when she and Rex met, the attraction was mutual. They appeared in plays and roamed the darkened streets of war-torn Britain together. A week's theatrical engagement in Liverpool sealed their romantic relationship and resulted in their own engagement.

Divorce from Colette was finalised in 1942 and marriage to Lili followed in 1943. This union also brought one son. He was given his grandmother's maiden name, Carey, as his first name.

Rex had an excessively jealous nature. If he thought anyone was too friendly with Lili he frequently made ugly scenes in public. For this, he was once thrown out of a restaurant in London. On another occasion he had a fight with Frank Sinatra, based on a silly misunderstanding. But it was Lili who had real cause for jealousy. Rex began an affair with a young starlet, Carole Landis. Worse still, he wasn't genuinely committed to the budding actress. Her suicide happened immediately after he ended their relationship. Ironically, at the time he was starring in a production called *Unfaithfully Yours*. When he was cast in the stage version of *Anna and the King of Siam*, he and the show were an instant success but other commitments prevented him from taking part in the film version.

At about this time, Rex's cousin, Joyce Carey, the sports mistress at Holly Lodge High School for Girls, in West Derby, Liverpool, often promised her pupils that the now-famous Rex would visit to coach them in tennis. Obligations in Hollywood and the West End, however, prevented this and the schoolgirls were always left disappointed.

The next relationship in Rex Harrison's life was with the lithe and entrancing Kay Kendall. She had similar qualities to Audrey Hepburn, his co-star in the film, *My Fair Lady*. Kay was fragile, graceful and appealed to every man she met, including Prince Carl of Sweden and James Sainsbury. Rex immediately felt protective towards her. When he discovered that her life was threatened by leukaemia, he felt compelled to care for her and shield her from the devastating truth. He begged Lili to divorce him so that he could marry Kay. Reluctantly, Lili complied, leaving Rex free to wed Kay and do everything in his power to make her happy and to prolong her life. Kay lived for another three years, never discovering the real cause of her permanent exhaustion. After her death, Rex hoped to remarry Lili but, understandably, Lili refused.

My Fair Lady was an enormous success. Harrison seemed the very epitome of the educated, self-assured professor. Behind the scenes it was a different story. He was prone to tremendous rages, stalking off the set and refusing to return. He became intensely unpopular. When he gave a party for the crew, nobody turned up. He began to realise his own shortcomings, saying, 'I'm at the age when I have to prove that I'm just as good as I never was.'

Rachel Thomas, another actress, came into his life. They were married for nine years, during which Rex filmed his other great success, *Doctor Dolittle*, but Rachel's alcoholic behaviour became increasingly scandalous and embarrassing until she was no longer in control of herself and she too committed suicide.

Elizabeth Harris had been married to Richard Harris, the film actor, and already had three sons when she and Rex wed in 1971. Again, the marriage was doomed and ended in 1975. She is quoted as saying, 'The way Rex eats a peach is positively pornographic.' 'Oh good,' was Rex's comment, 'so she can say some nice things about me then!'

By 1978, Rex was married again, to the much younger Mercia Tinker. Like Henry VIII, his sixth wife outlived him. Before that, in 1989, he was knighted by Her Majesty Queen Elizabeth II while an orchestra played tunes from *My Fair Lady*.

Many people adored him. Many abhorred him. Many people idolised him from afar, but when they met him, their feelings often changed. One winter's night, in the wind and rain, a little old lady waited outside the stage door to ask for his autograph. Irritably, he told her to 'sod off!'

Stanley Holloway came out of the theatre, just in time to see the old dear smack Rex with her theatre programme. 'Well, well,' said Stanley, 'that's the first time I've ever seen the fan hit the shit!'

Frank Hornby 1863–1936

The Meccano Man

Several generations of children, mostly boys, have enjoyed the construction toy Meccano and have learned from it the basics of mechanical engineering. Their imaginations have been stretched and their education greatly improved while they thought they were just having fun. The inventor of this world-famous toy, Frank Hornby, was born at 77 Copperas Hill, Liverpool, into a happy and tight-knit family which was eventually to include seven children. As a youngster, Frank found the Liverpool Docks fascinating. He loved seeing the huge cranes winching up the cargoes on to the ocean-going ships and liners. He enjoyed the bustling atmosphere of sailors and passengers preparing to set sail for ports across the Irish Sea and the Atlantic Ocean and he envisaged the excitement of setting foot on foreign soil.

Although a bright pupil, Frank's education was somewhat pedestrian. It prepared him for neither an academic nor a technical career. Initially, a lowly clerical job was the limit of his expectations. He was accepted into the offices of a Mr David Elliot at 12 Duke Street in the heart of Liverpool. There he remained for many years. For some, such a humdrum, almost Dickensian occupation might have been stultifying but, while learning book-keeping and business administration, Frank's imagination was constantly at work. He had a dream which he was determined to turn into reality. He wanted to create some sort of kit which would mimic the constructional engineering of the adult world.

Frank lived during a period when educationalists from several Western countries were beginning to realise the benefits of educational toys and he was keen to make a plaything that could be used in many different ways. His idea was that a child could take pleasure in constructing one object, play with it for a while, but when the possibilities of that version had been exhausted, the component parts could be separated and then reassembled into something entirely different. Today, this concept does not seem in any way exceptional, as many toys are built on this principle, but no one had thought of it before Frank Hornby. He envisaged miniature forms of his long-time favourite cranes being easily transformed into bridges, moving railway signals and even locomotives. He particularly wanted the components to be sturdy, unbreakable and reusable. While this ambitious aspiration was still trapped inside his head, he had to begin with the more mundane process of finding the raw materials. His preference was for something metallic. In the experimental stages, he cut small strips from biscuit tins and perforated these with evenly spaced holes. He then needed screws, nuts and bolts to hold the interchangeable sections together. Such locking devices proved difficult to obtain, so the obvious solution was to make them himself.

Having found himself a charming and well-educated wife who was sympathetic to his aspirations, they moved from their respective parental homes into a house of their own. In the back garden, Frank built himself a suitable shed and proceeded to fit it out as his own little workshop. Many happy evenings were spent there after office hours, experimenting until he felt ready to proceed to the next stage.

From nine to five, Hornby was an exemplary employee, hardworking and more than competent. He even made sure that he looked the part. Rather than the eccentricities associated with some inventive geniuses, Frank dressed like the archetypal civil servant, stiff white collar, bow tie, formal suit, fob watch and a waxed moustache. Over the years, he became irreplaceable to his boss. His natural progression was to chief clerk. Chatting to Mr Elliot during lunch hours and tea breaks, Hornby was able to formulate his ideas and was delighted to discover that Elliot took a friendly interest in his schemes. The first advantage from this good working relationship was the fact that Elliot allowed Hornby to use a section of the business premises to experiment. As Hornby's plans showed signs of potential success, Elliot understood the need to protect the idea. He lent Frank the necessary £5 to register the product with the Patent Office. This freed up some of Hornby's own savings to purchase metal parts from professional firms. Progress was definitely being made, but not without some difficulties. Because the various parts were being supplied by different firms, the measurements did not always match the units from other sources.

At home, the family was growing, a much longed-for baby girl was eventually to join Frank and Clara's two sons. But with a helpful boss and a wife who was prepared to make ends meet, on what was left over after all experimental expenses had been met, Hornby was able to progress.

As he had never had the benefit of an engineering training, he knew that he must consult qualified mechanics and engineers. He was lucky enough to find Henry Selby Hele-Shaw, the first ever professor of engineering at Liverpool University. Testament to Hele-Shaw's inventive brilliance, an aeroplane propeller and a motor car clutch were later named after him. The advice and instruction Hornby received from this talented mentor helped enormously in the development of 'Mechanics Made Easy – an Adaptable and Mechanical Toy', as Hornby initially called his product.

It was now time to start marketing. In those days, toys were not the big business of the twentieth and twenty-first centuries. They were sold on street corners and at country fairs. So that was how Hornby began. With slow but steady progress, he was able at first, to repay the £5 loan, then rent the premises next door to Elliott's office in Duke Street. Eventually, at 18 James Street, he was able to afford one female employee and then persuade the educational retailer, Phillip, Son and Nephew, to start selling the boxed outfits on a commercial basis.

Hornby soon became adept at publicising his product. He knew that items were not likely to become famous of their own accord. Fortunately, he had natural entrepreneurial skills. He was one of the first manufacturers to realise that competitions generate sales. Prizes were awarded to children who could design and assemble structures different from every other model. The response was overwhelming. Entries came from school groups as well as individuals. Another inspired promotional stratagem was a magazine dedicated to Meccano, as the kits were now known. This became a huge success and engendered loyalty for many years. Not only were there illustrations and instructions for intricate developments, but fans were encouraged to write news letters or ask for advice. Friendships were formed, pen-pals corresponded and specialist journalists were engaged to offer guidance on possible careers.

Sales and profits grew rapidly. Frank soon realised that he could expand into foreign markets. He introduced his product into France, Germany and Holland. America proved to have enormous potential and Frank was keen to act as his own very successful sales representative. Over the coming years, he crossed the Atlantic more than sixty times, and the English Channel so often that he lost count. Meccano fever even spread to Canada, Africa and the Far East.

Of course, Hornby no longer worked for Elliot but the £5 had been repaid many times over. Elliot made shrewd investments as the company grew, so both men benefited from their association. Clara and the children were not neglected either. Clara had given up teaching long before, her love of music was indulged in every way and Mr and Mrs Frank Hornby still went dancing whenever possible. Their sons, Roland and Douglas attended the Liverpool Institute. The boys later studied in France and Germany. After serving in the First World War, they helped to expand the business.

Then great sadness affected the Hornby family; Frank and Clara were travelling abroad when their much-loved daughter, Patricia, died suddenly at the age of fourteen from Poliomyelitis. The loss was devastating and her parents never fully recovered.

In 1914, Meccano had expanded so much that the factory was able to move into purpose-built premises in Binns Road, where it remained for sixty years, housing between two and three thousand male and female workers.

In 1931, Frank, having created employment for so many local people, became the MP for Everton. But his easy days were over. He faced a difficult battle during the years of Depression, both as a politician and as a businessman. Competitors were producing similar kits, using newer, plastic materials. Fresh ideas were being fostered all over Europe to find devices to outdo Frank's kits. Meccano diversified into Dinky Toys, miniature replicas of every type of road vehicle. Fortunately, these too became immensely popular and are still collectors' items. Hornby Trains, another of Meccano's all-time favourites, have never lost their appeal. Grown men still have attics or cellars entirely occupied by their model train sets. Today, although Meccano is no longer made in this country, the hobby has many fervent enthusiasts. Enter the word into any internet search engine and you can take your choice of dozens of spare parts, specialist pieces or even that one particular wing screw needed to complete the most intricate construction. Meccano is alive and well and living in boys' bedrooms all over the modern world. Not only that, but professional architects and engineers save immense amounts of money, time and effort by expressing their visions in Meccano, making adaptations and demonstrating their concepts to colleagues before embarking on the final multi-million pound realisation.

Mention the words Binns Road in Liverpool and a nostalgic smile spreads across the face of many a senior citizen who took such pride in helping to manufacture one of the most enjoyable educational toys ever.

Jeremiah Horrocks 1619–41

Child Prodigy and Youthful 'Father' of British Astronomy

en are from Mars. Women are from Venus. So the saying goes. Venus was the Roman goddess of beauty. As the mother of Cupid, she is also associated with love. One brilliantly gifted young Liverpudlian loved the planet Venus in an intellectual way. He was also fascinated by all planets and had a strong desire to further scientific knowledge about the solar system.

Galileo, the world famous Italian astronomer, born in 1564, was fifty-four years of age when Jeremiah Horrocks was born in Toxteth in 1618. Galileo lived to be seventy-seven and died in 1642 but young Horrocks died in 1641, at the very early age of twenty-three. Had he lived, Jeremiah Horrocks may well have rivalled Galileo in scientific discoveries concerning the characteristics and movements of the bodies in the solar system.

Until the latter half of the seventeenth century, the accepted truth concerning the Earth and the sun was that the Earth was static and the sun moved around it. Galileo's studies caused him to dispute the accuracy of this belief and he set out to prove the truth of his theories. He was a mathematician, a scientist, an astronomer and a philosopher. He was also a professor at two universities. He developed telescopes to improve the ability to study the night sky but his revolutionary claims were met with hostility from the established Church of Rome. This was because his assertions contradicted accepted traditions which the Church believed should never be questioned. Jeremiah Horrocks also challenged historical inaccuracies and made progress in the field of scientific knowledge, although he followed a different mode of study and experiment from Galileo.

Even as a child, Jeremiah showed signs of intellectual brilliance. Born into a family of watchmakers, situated on what were then the rural outskirts of Liverpool at Toxteth Park, his childhood was that of a country boy, familiar with the woodlands, deer and windmills of the locality but still within walking distance of the town which, at that time, consisted of only seven streets. Familiarity with the component parts used in watchmaking, especially the glass, would help Jeremiah, in adulthood, to improve upon the extremely primitive telescopes of the day.

Jeremiah's earliest education was at Toxteth Ancient Chapel, where his aptitude for learning soon became apparent. He outshone all other pupils in Mathematics, science and Latin. He also showed great appreciation of the poetry of William Shakespeare who had died just two years before Jeremiah was born.

At the tender age of fourteen, Jeremiah left the North-West and made the week-long journey to the eastern side of England to study at Emmanuel College, Cambridge. He continued his Latin, scientific and mathematical education and formed good friendships with his fellow undergraduates. During vacations, the teenage student returned to Merseyside and sometimes visited friends at Hoole,

An oil painting depicting Jeremiah Horrocks in 1639, with his successful experiment to capture the first ever image of the transit of Venus across the sun.

about 18 miles north of Toxteth on what is now the A59. In those days the roads were so poor it was easier to go on horseback, along the shoreline of the Mersey Estuary via the firm, white beaches of Blundellsands, Formby, Ainsdale and Southport. The long, unbroken stretches of sand were ideal for a brisk gallop. There were no protruding rocks, only the beautiful dunes and pinewoods bordering the inland side. The tidal ebbs and flows along the route were also a source of fascination to Jeremiah and he began to wonder about the influence of heavenly bodies upon the Earth's daily patterns. These visits to Hoole helped him to realise what a perfect view of the skies could be obtained from this area. He hoped for a much longer stay when his studies were complete.

After he graduated, Jeremiah spent three years in the family business but this was not stimulating nor demanding enough for such a genius. With his father's blessing, he continued his observations and experiments at Carr House, Hoole. He was still too young and studious to find a sweetheart but he did have a romantic nature. He wrote poetry to rival Shakespeare's blank verse. He serenaded Venus as if she were his fiancée, begging her to stay longer rather than continue her journey to other lands.

Where dost thou madly hasten? Oh! Return:
Such barbarous lands can never duly hail
The purer brightness of thy virgin light.
Or rather here remain: secure from harm,
Thy bed we'll strew with all the fairest flowers:
Refresh thy frame, by labours seldom tried,
Too much oppressed; and let that gentle form
Recline in safety on the friendly couch.

Jeremiah built a model to illustrate the movements of the planets. He suggested that the planets could have far-reaching effects upon each other (as indeed the moon affects the earth's tides) and he was in the vanguard of scientists contradicting the age-old view that the Earth was the centre of the universe. Jeremiah's greatest achievement was constructing a device by which he could track the movements of the planet Venus across the face of the sun. He correctly calculated that this could be seen in Europe on 24 November 1639. As telescopes were still in their infancy, he made his own, far superior version. He drew three diagrams of the sun on three separate pieces of card then drew narrow sections through the angles of the circles to form an asterisk-shaped grid. From a bedroom window at Carr House, he waited for the perfect moment. He was not disappointed. Via an image projected from his telescope, he witnessed a dark circle which moved across the facsimile of the sun, projected onto the first card. Twenty minutes later, after the dark spot had moved, he substituted the next card and recorded the planet's new position. Twenty minutes after that he repeated the procedure, thus proving that the dark spot, Venus, was moving across the sun.

Nowadays, in the twenty-first century, with the benefit of computers, calculators, vast telescopes and immediate worldwide electronic communications, this may seem primitive, almost child-like. Horrocks was hardly out of his teens. Sophisticated equipment was totally undreamt of, the workings of the universe were still being explained in the form of myths, legends, superstition and bigoted religious dogmas. No one had previously troubled to obtain such scientific proof. Horrocks was working without assistance and could not have been in the best of health as he died only a year after his revolutionary discovery. Under these circumstances his achievement was phenomenal.

The sun over the Mersey Estuary set early on that November afternoon. The sun set early on the life of this young Liverpudlian genius but his dedication advanced the course of scientific knowledge to the benefit of all generations to come. His discovery and proof are known as 'The Transit of Venus.'

Geoffrey Hughes

The 'Lazy Slob' who Never Stops Working!

Do you recognise this neat young man with the intelligent eyes and the clean-shaven, modest smile? Maybe it's a little while since you have seen him looking quite as presentable as this. If your memory is good, you may recall him emptying a few bins into the refuse lorries outside the terraced houses of *Coronation Street*. Or trying unsuccessfully to help Jim Royle with a bit of slap-dash painting and laminating to impress Barbara and her Mam. What about Vernon Scripps, always up to some dodgy deal near the Yorkshire Moors?

Very likely your mental image of him includes Hyacinth Bucket's total embarrassment of a brother-in-law, sloppy, slovenly Onslow, lying in bed all day surrounded by empty beer cans and greasy chip papers. His total command of the English language at that time appeared to be restricted to the sardonic use of the word 'Nice!'

Well think again. Never judge a book by its cover. Inside all these shiftless characters hides the successful and workaholic actor, Geoffrey Hughes. Over a period of forty years, in a difficult business, as well as appearing on stage and in film, he has played significant parts in four long-running and highly acclaimed television series. This, of course, entails extremely long hours; up at six, uncomfortable conditions on location in all weathers and the ability to learn a new set of lines and moves every week. Looking like a lazy idiot requires plenty of brains, stamina and dedication.

Between working on soap operas and sitcoms, Geoffrey is also a Shakespearian actor, having played Pistil in *Henry V* and Trinculo in *The Tempest*. He has also appeared in *Doctor Who* as well as in the film version of Leslie Thomas's *The Virgin Soldiers* and in *The Man from the Pru*, the true story of the Florence Maybrick murder in Liverpool. He once provided the voice of Paul McCartney in the cartoon version of *The Yellow Submarine*. Nearly every Christmas, he takes on the arduous task of entertaining excited youngsters who fill huge theatres to see live pantomime. He has also sung on television, once as Twiggy in *The Royle Family* and once in an opera called *Good Friday 1663*.

While touring Australia in a stage play, he was invited to speak to a Ladies' Literary Group about *Keeping up Appearances*. Nearly all 500 of them turned up looking like Hyacinth Bucket. It wasn't fancy dress! It was their natural choice of outfit.

Geoffrey was born in Kirkdale but when he was six his family moved to Norris Green, where he spent his formative years. He attended Westminster Road School, hen those at Ranworth Square and Abbotsford Road. When he left school at sixteen, he worked for a while for the John Lewis Partnership before going to London to try his hand at the performing arts.

'As a struggling actor,' he recalls, 'I once took a temporary job selling ice cream at the Chelsea Flower Show. I must have done it well because at the end of the week they offered me a permanent position as an ice cream sales rep. Some people say I gave up a promising career.'

During his early days in show business, Geoffrey was once voted most promising newcomer by the readers of the *Daily Express*, 'And then I was out of work for the next four months,' he says, ruefully. 'The only other accolade I ever received,' he adds, 'was when a journalist said that I had raised slobbery to an art form. I'm not sure whether that was a compliment or not!'

'I think the most stimulating part I ever played was Vladimir in *Waiting For Godot*. I always went on stage knowing what I was going to do, thinking I could see the "line" threading through the piece but I always came off feeling depressed, as if I'd lost it somewhere during the performance. A great play. I think it's the nature of Beckett that he picks up actors, shakes them about and then throws them down like a piece of wet rag. It's a play you could never become tired of performing, if only for the belief that one day you might get it right.'

Geoffrey plays golf in his spare time. Judging by the above comments, it sounds as though golf and *Waiting For Godot* have something in common!

As well as enjoying the challenge of serious drama, Geoffrey certainly has happy memories of playing Eddie Yeats from 1974 to 1983, Onslow from 1990 to 1996, then straight on to becoming Twiggy from 1996 until 2006 with the opportunity between episodes of *The Royle Family* to strut his style as Vernon Scripps from 2000 to 2004 in *Heartbeat*.

If you met any of these characters as real people you might not want them as your best friend but Geoffrey, the actor, is so different. In private life, he says he tries to be aware of the environment and is a patron of the Red Squirrel Trust on the Isle of Wight. 'Having been a sufferer myself, the charity closest to my . . . I nearly said "heart" but I probably should have said "loins", is the Prostate Cancer Charity. Thankfully there is much more awareness of the problem in the male population these days.' For a change, in December 2007, Geoffrey became quite an angel. The Angel Gabriel, in fact, in the live, open-air televised version of the *Liverpool Nativity*. Geoffrey was in effect the Master of Ceremonies, narrator and link-man for the whole performance. In modern dress, he was joined by fellow Liverpudlian thespians, Cathy Tyson as Herodia; Paul McGann, David Yip, and Louis Emerick as the three wise men; Gerry Marsden as the Ferry Man and Jennifer Ellison as the leading choir angel. The inn where there was no room was played by the Dr Duncan Pub, owned by Liverpool's main brewery, Cains. Geoffrey and the whole cast brought the message of the age-old story right into the twenty-first century.

Glenda Jackson

The Only British MP to Have Won Two Oscars

Members of Parliament are not often noted for their sense of humour, whereas members of the theatrical profession are. Glenda Jackson's star sign must surely be Gemini, the twins, as two balanced but different facets of her personality complement each other perfectly. In each of her vocations both thespian and political, she has been equally dedicated, equally good humoured and equally highly regarded.

During her theatrical, film and television career, Glenda Jackson played many parts. In response to questions concerning the emotional demands of her wide-ranging roles, she explained 'When I have to cry, I think of my love life. When I have to laugh, I think of my love life.'

Here is a woman, multi-talented, with a background of Shakespearian and other classical productions, who relished the opportunity to carry on a little tomfoolery with Morecambe and Wise, in comedy sketches written by Liverpudlian Eddie Brabin, which she achieved with great gusto.

Glenda was born on the Wirral side of the Mersey and attended West Kirkby Grammar School for Girls. She left school at sixteen and, for two years, worked in a branch of Boots the Chemist. 'You know,' she muses, 'If I'd played my cards right, I

could have been an area manager for Boots by now.' Years later, when she appeared in an advertisement for Boots products, she gave her fee to a children's charity.

When she was a student at RADA (the Royal Academy of Dramatic Arts) money was in short supply. 'Each week, I used to live on a pound of sausages and a baking apple. I used to empty other people's ashtrays and use the cigarette butts to roll into fags for myself.'

In 1958, she married and subsequently had a son. She has not remarried since her divorce in 1976.

During Ken Russell's erotic film *The Music Lovers*, Glenda was five months pregnant so, in the nude scenes, she was confident that her bosom was the best it had ever been!

From the early days of her acting career, Glenda's rich and expressive voice has been a wonderful asset. Her mellifluous diction and strong stage and screen presence have brought her a wealth of parts and several best actress awards including those from the national film critics, the New York film critics and the Academy Awards, plus two Emmy Awards, the Etoile de Cristale from France and the British CBE.

Glenda is not particularly impressed by show business trophies. However, this didn't stop her giving many outstanding performances in her moving portrayals of complex women. The list is impressive: Lady Macbeth, Salome, Hedda Gabler, Joan of Arc, Sarah Bernhardt, Gudrun Brangwen, Mary Queen of Scots, Roald Dahl's American film star wife Patricia Neal and Tchaikovsky's nymphomaniac wife, as well as that gift to all serious actresses, Queen Elizabeth I.

In the film *Business As Usual*, set in Liverpool, Glenda took the role of the real-life manageress of a fashion boutique, the victim of unfair dismissal following her support of a younger shop assistant subjected to sexual harassment. Another biographical film was based on the true life story of a historical near-neighbour of Glenda's, Emma, Lady Hamilton, the mistress of Admiral Lord Nelson. Emma Hamilton was born at Hawarden, close to Wirral.

In contrast to so many dramatic characters, on the *Morecambe and Wise Show*, Cleopatra was played entirely for laughs and was a huge television success. These are just a few of Glenda's outstanding performances. Having played just about every emotionally demanding female character ever written to huge critical acclaim, Glenda decided to devote more time to her other all-abiding interest, politics. She felt that the time was right to make a graceful exit from show business and to turn her attention to the challenges of helping others.

In 1992, Ms Jackson was elected as the Labour MP for Hampstead and Highgate. In 1997, Tony Blair appointed her as Junior Minister with special responsibility for London Transport. In order to be nominated for Mayor of London in the year 2000, it was necessary to resign her ministerial post. Although unsuccessful, she accepted Ken Livingstone's invitation to become an adviser in his 'cabinet' with special responsibility concerning homelessness. She also tackles problems such as poverty, unemployment and environmental issues. Other matters giving her concern are the number of young people who feel disadvantaged and disengaged from today's mainstream society and, conversely, the hundreds of pensioners afraid to go out after dark because they fear those very same teenagers.

As a highly successful professional woman herself, Ms Jackson is a champion of women's advancement. She hates the 'glass ceiling' and sees no reason why a woman's appearance should have any more bearing on her suitability for a high-ranking post than a man's does. At the same time, she deplores the fact that some women claim they never vote. With good reason, she feels that, as some suffragettes gave their lives to achieve equality and universal suffrage, subsequent generations have a duty to avail themselves of that right. In 2003, Ms Jackson made clear her disapproval of the invasion of Iraq. She also called for the then Prime Minister's resignation over the question of the death of Dr David Kelly, the man who threw doubt on the existence of Saddam's weapons of mass destruction.

With the wide-ranging experience of all the characters she has ever portrayed, many of them historically authentic, stored away in her memory, added to her own innate sagacity, the Honourable Member for Hampstead and Highgate, CBE is well placed to use her eloquent powers of persuasion in the service of her constituents and the country in general.

Sir Robert Jones 1858–1933

Surgeon, Gentleman and Gentle Man

When Hugh Owen Thomas was about forty, his fifteen-year-old nephew, Robert Jones, arrived to live with him and to learn from him. Robert, born in Rhyl, was gifted with the same fervent interest in medical matters, especially anything concerning the bones, joints and limbs. How fortunate, then, that middle-aged Hugh Owen Thomas and schoolboy Robert Jones were so compatible in their devotion to patients and to remedial innovation.

In every other way, however, they were complete opposites. Uncle Hugh, the puny, irritable, control freak, unsociable, careless of his personal appearance, always at odds with everyone in his profession, was respected only by the underprivileged for whom he worked so ardently. How forbearing the teenage Robert must have been to tolerate such an eccentric taskmaster. Robert had a sunny nature, and was warm-hearted, humorous, well-mannered and charismatic in every way. Moreover, he was perceptive. He could see what the 'high and mighty' refused to acknowledge. He understood his uncle's experiments. Willingly, he assisted in manipulating sprained or deformed limbs and dislocated joints. He admired his uncle's inventions, helped to fit the strange new splints and agreed with the principle of healing the poor in preference to the over-indulged rich. Indeed he became his uncle's disciple.

Robert had a boyish charm and always looked younger than his actual age. In fact, some patients felt he might be too inexperienced. They were nervous at putting themselves at his mercy. But he proved to be an able pupil and made rapid progress, even studying midwifery for a while in Dublin, the Mecca of this subject at the time. At the appropriate age, Robert enrolled at the Liverpool Medical School and studied there for the next six years. When he qualified, he went straight back to the Nelson Street Surgery and continued as his uncle's colleague, still absorbing ideas and building up practical experience. After he was appointed Honorary Assistant at Stanley Hospital, Liverpool, the time came for him to move on. He bought a property in Great George Square and set up his own practice.

Two important events occurred in 1887. Firstly, Robert found romance and married Susie Evans, with whom he eventually had two children. Secondly, work on the Manchester Ship Canal was started. This was a huge project, taking six years to complete. During that time, three thousand injuries were recorded. With such hazards, three hospitals were needed, one at each end of the canal and another halfway along. Robert Jones was appointed as the consultant surgeon, working on site while at the same time, training others in fracture care, management efficiency and the application of his uncle's splints.

Robert never severed his association with his uncle. They continued to work together until Hugh Owen Thomas's untimely death in 1891. Robert then took over the Nelson Street Surgery and assumed some of his predecessor's working practices. Up at the crack of dawn, twenty-six operations per day and free surgeries on Sundays. His patient list rose to about 7,000 every year. He made sure that orthopaedic surgery, ignored for so long, received the recognition it deserved.

Unlike his reclusive uncle, Robert managed to combine all this with a very active social life. He loved giving generous dinner parties, he went riding and shooting and played cricket. Oddly for one so celebrated in the curing of injuries, he became an amateur pugilist. It was only when his boxing skills knocked out one opponent that Robert realised boxing was best treated as a spectator sport.

Always popular, always genial, Robert quickly put everyone at their ease. He attracted large numbers of child patients and was keen to improve the quality of life for young cripples. He built on his uncle's methods, used his uncle's famous 'Thomas Splint' and spread the idea of the curative properties of fresh air and leisure activities. Robert himself was an experimenter. With his colleague, Thurston Holland, he was the first to make use of an x-ray, when asked to locate a bullet lodged in the wrist of a young boy.

In 1899, Robert's expertise was recognised by his appointment as general surgeon at the Royal Southern Hospital, Liverpool. The following year, one of his patients was Agnes Hunt, a nurse from Baschurch in Shropshire. During her childhood in Australia she had suffered from osteomyelitis following septicaemia. A painful hip brought her to Liverpool to seek treatment from Robert Jones. The two found that they had ideas and ideals in common. She too had a strong belief in fresh air and plenty of play-time for child patients. Nurse Hunt persuaded Mr Jones to visit her Home for Crippled Children in Baschurch. He was impressed with what he saw and made frequent visits to monitor the progress of the children. Ultimately, between them they created the first children's orthopaedic hospital in the world. More Robert Jones and Agnes Hunt Homes were opened, all with operating theatres, schoolrooms, well-stocked play areas and outdoor leisure facilities. Agnes steadily gained a reputation as an important authority on the care of crippled children.

Robert continued with his campaign to widen the scope of treatment for the musculo-skeletal system, challenging those doctors who still considered orthopaedics as just another aspect of general surgery. By 1905, he had decided to concentrate only on orthopaedics and wrote widely on the subject. His forward-thinking hope of all large cities having hospitals with separate accident and emergency departments were far in advance of the custom at that time.

It was during Robert's tenure at the Royal Southern that young Noel Chavasse (see p. 16) joined his unit and became a welcome addition to Robert's team. Robert became Noel's mentor. It was a association of great benefit to Noel's understanding and practical expertise in orthopaedics, and a liaison which was to last for the rest of Noel's life.

At the outbreak of the First World War, despite jealous objections from London-based doctors, the War Office appointed Robert Jones as Major General Inspector of Military Orthopaedics. His letters with advice and encouragement to Captain Noel Chavasse were of supreme importance to Noel when he was saving lives in the heat of battle.

Robert's guidance to the military on the use of his uncle's invention, the 'Thomas Splint' had startlingly beneficial results. Deaths in the trenches due to multiple fractures were reduced from 80 per cent to 20 per cent within a short space of time. Robert worked tirelessly throughout the war, becoming a captain in the RAMC. His engaging personality never deserted him. At one point during his military service, he was called to a protracted squabble between the British and the Swiss authorities on internment. Within three days, the iceberg of confrontation had melted and Robert had settled the whole situation to everyone's satisfaction. 'Jones,' said one of his compatriots, 'you are wasted in medicine – you should have been an ambassador!'

Reward in the form of a CBE and then a knighthood came in 1917 and 1919. Sir Robert Jones never lost his flair as a writer, lecturer and educator. His enlightened attitudes have influenced subsequent generations even to the present day. His work resulted in the founding of the Central Council for the Care of Cripples.

His abiding energy and charm were acknowledged when, after his funeral in 1933, his ashes were laid to rest in the Chapel of Service at Liverpool Cathedral, where a memorial stone was placed. 'For him, the thread of life was strung with the precious beads of thought and love.'

In recognition of her visionary dedication, Agnes Hunt (1886–1946) was created a Dame of the British Empire in 1926.

When researching the details of the lives and careers of Dr Hugh Owen Thomas, Sir Robert Jones and Nurse Agnes Hunt, at the Liverpool Medical Institute, I walked into the reception area holding a photocopy of two portraits featuring the above doctors. A lady I had not noticed previously said 'Oh, you've got a picture of Sir Robert Jones. I'm Joanna Whitely, his great-great-granddaughter. I'm doing a PhD and who better to study than my great-great-grandfather?' Dr Hugh Owen Thomas and Sir Robert Jones would be so delighted to know that yet another generation, Joanna's daughter, is studying to become a doctor.

Margaret Kelly 1910–2004

Miss Bluebell

This book contains mini-biographies of many Merseysiders who rose from modest beginnings to find fame and fortune by their own talents and enthusiasm for hard work. None could have come from humbler origins than the celebrated Parisienne, Miss Bluebell. Parisienne? Well, that was what she had become by the end of the Second World War.

Originally, this nameless orphan never knew who her biological parents were. She never knew her real surname and had no background support of loving grandparents or relations of any sort. 'Kelly' was supposed to be her family name, but what parent would give truthful details of a baby about to be abandoned? 'Margaret' was the name chosen by the Liverpudlian nurse who adopted her when the Catholic Church in Ireland needed to find homes for weak and unwanted babies.

Nurse Maureen Murphy brought the sickly infant across the Irish Sea to her home in Deysbrook Lane, West Derby, Liverpool. Thanks to the capable care of this loving spinster, Margaret survived. Her adoptive mother gave her a roof over her head, plain but wholesome nourishment and warm, home-made clothes. In spite of all this, the child still needed frequent medical attention. When she was about five, one doctor was particularly taken with her pale complexion and beautiful blue eyes. Hearing the tale of her nameless background, he remarked that she should have been christened Bluebell, especially as her spindly legs were as thin as flower stalks. The little girl was flattered by the nickname and insisted on using it from then on.

It was on medical advice that she was enrolled in a local dance class, as a form of physiotherapy to strengthen her muscles. It soon became apparent that she had a flair for dancing. She enjoyed dancing so much that it became an important part of her life. Money was scarce in this one-parent household, so Bluebell insisted on paying her own way by helping the milkman, doing paper deliveries and caddying at the nearby West Derby golf course. Tough work for a fragile and now-gangly child.

But her resilience improved as she became a tall and slender pre-teen. As soon as it was legal for her to do so, she left school. At fourteen, she joined a professional dance troupe. In those days, before television, any theatrical job entailed touring, staying in cheap digs and fending for oneself in all weathers. Bluebell quickly developed a spirit of independence and an instinct for self-preservation. In fact, after seeing most of the country, including Scotland, she soon ventured further afield with a dance troupe working in Berlin. This was the era in which the musicals *Cabaret* and *Chicago* are set, so it is easy to picture the kind of life into which this innocent young dancer was plunged. She stayed for about five years. In doing do, she learned the language, began to understand the way of life and the way German people viewed the world.

When the troupe visited Paris, Bluebell fell in love with the place and stayed on to try her luck. Because of her long legs, good figure and obvious ability, Bluebell found it easy to join the world famous Folies Bergère. This, and the rival Moulin Rouge and Lido nightclubs had always had a reputation for being the sauciest and most glamorous venues in Europe. So successful, in fact, that their style has been copied in Las Vegas and in the Far East. Bluebell quickly rose from the chorus line to become principal dancer. By the time she was twenty-two, she was ready to form her own company, a line-up known to this day as the Bluebell Girls. Although situated in Paris, many Bluebell girls are British, because Miss Bluebell considered British-trained dancers to be better disciplined and more co-operative. Bluebell preferred classically trained dancers, especially those who had grown too tall for conventional ballet companies. Long legs were essential for her stylish shows. Her criteria were, 'Height not less than 5ft 9in, long legs, high, well-formed derrières, firm breasts but not too large and definitely not dangling.'

Romance came into Bluebell's life when she met the gifted and good-looking pianist at the Folies Bergère, Marcel Leibovici. He was Romanian, of Jewish descent and their mutual attraction was immediate and lasting. They were soon married and expecting a baby.

But this was 1939. Hitler invaded Poland. Germany was now Bluebell's enemy and France was thrown into turmoil. The newly married Mr and Mrs Leibovici realised they should leave France but they delayed too long before attempting to sail for England. The Nazis reached Paris. It wasn't safe to have a Jewish or a British surname. Miss Bluebell, Mrs Margaret Leibovici, was interned by the Nazis and her husband was arrested for no reason except his nationality. Deportation and eventually the gas chamber awaited him in Germany. En route, somewhere near Switzerland, he managed to escape and thanks to his command of various languages, was able to make the long and dangerous journey back to Paris.

Because her papers proved that she was Irish-born, Margaret was eventually released from internment. When she learned that Marcel had escaped, she was delighted. But her delight was short-lived. She discovered that he was hiding in a building where the receptionist was a known collaborator who had betrayed many Jewish people to the Nazis.

'Margaret' became 'Bluebell' again and her enterprising instinct for self-preservation took over. She used her initiative to find all sorts of 'luxury' items such as eggs, meat and coffee. All of these, Bluebell used as bribes for the concièrge. Astonishingly, the woman kept the secret and greedily accepted the bribes. Even so, there were many heart-stopping moments. On one occasion, Bluebell was taken to the Gestapo headquarters and questioned. Her knowledge of German helped her to convince the authorities that she had no idea where her husband was. The fact that she was pregnant again was a stumbling block but, being a showgirl, it was easy to give the impression that she had another lover.

The nightmare of deception continued for years but against all odds, Marcel's life was saved and the couple eventually had two sons and a daughter. When Paris was liberated, both took out French naturalisation papers.

Budding Bluebell Girls practise posing outside Miss
Bluebell's cottage in Deysbrook Lane, West Derby.

Bluebell Girls show their affection for Ken Dodd.

In peacetime, Bluebell teamed up with Donn Arden, who choreographed and directed shows at the Lido. As at the other leading nightclubs, the shows became more and more lavish. Dancers were of the highest calibre, costumes were almost non-existent but the feathered head-dresses were fancy and colourful. The scenery was dazzling, often incorporating waterfalls and pools into which acrobatic dancers would dive and glide. Skaters performed on ice, there were aerial numbers where swings swept out over the audience. Ticket sales soared. The huge auditorium was always packed.

In spite of the risqué reputation of the spectacular shows, Miss Bluebell insisted on the highest propriety of her girls. She had seen the innuendo in the paintings of Dégas and she wouldn't allow any scandal to be attached to her protégées. Marcel composed songs for Edith Piaf and music for the highly successful shows. Bluebell and her husband now belonged to the champagne set and lived on the Champs Elysees. But after preserving his life all through the war, Bluebell did lose her beloved Marcel in 1961, when he died in a car accident.

Because she was now officially French, Bluebell's honours were the Legion de Merite, the Chevalier des Arts et Lettres and the Legion d'Honneur. But Britain didn't forget her. She also received the OBE and in 1986, the BBC serialised her life story, paying particular attention to the anxieties of the war years.

The sickly little orphan with no name grew up to become world famous and live to an active ninety-four years of age.

Bill Kenwright

The Man Who Always Knows the Score!

As well as being a musical buff and an ardent sports fan, Bill Kenwright is also an all-round good sport. At the turn of 2008, he took the opportunity to raise money for his favourite charities by competing in ITV's *Who Wants To Be A Millionaire?* and on the BBC's celebrity version of *Mastermind*. In the latter, he showed an amazing recall and depth of knowledge of the popular music of recent decades. During his introduction, he revealed to John Humphrys how his two contrasting great passions happened to collide.

'When I was a soccer-mad teenager,' he explained, 'I was disappointed when a local football match was cancelled. But, from a bus, I noticed the posters for a musical at the Empire Theatre in Lime Street. *West Side Story* looked interesting, so I bought a ticket for that instead. I was bowled over with the brilliance of the music and choreography. I immediately became just as keen on show business as I was on football.'

He has loved musicals ever since and has always adored football. His business acumen is also second to none. He is, above all others, the man who definitely knows the score!

From his home in Mossley Hill, the talented young Bill attended primary school at Booker Avenue, later moving on to the Liverpool Institute for Boys, now appropriately transformed into the Liverpool Institute for the Performing Arts. In the 1960s Bill formed a pop group, Bill Kenwright and the Runaways. Together they recorded a number of original pop tunes. In the same decade, Bill decided to try his hand at acting. Although he had no theatrical training, his good looks soon brought him parts in television shows such as *Z-Cars*, *The Villains* and *The Liver Birds*. In *Coronation Street*, he quickly gained popularity as Gordon Clegg, the adopted son of barmaid Betty Turpin at the Rover's Return. He stayed for about a year until his character took off for the bright lights of London. Whether art imitated life or vice versa, Bill himself did the same.

During the 1970s, he began to take an interest in the production and business side of London theatres. He became the director of two famously successful Andrew Lloyd Webber and Tim Rice shows, *Joseph And The Amazing Technicolour Dreamcoat* and *Jesus Christ Superstar*, as well as *Whistle Down The Wind* and Willy Russell's abiding triumph, *Blood Brothers*. All have had changes of cast and theatres and, with national touring companies, are still immensely successful. The Empire Theatre has played host to the shows, not once but many times over the years and still the audiences come by the coachload.

Bill's phenomenal business perspicacity made it possible for him to buy a major share in his favourite football team, Everton. He was initially invited to become Deputy Chairman, rising to Chairman in 2004. He is such an ardent supporter of the Toffees that he regularly journeys up from his business interests in London to

Bill Kenwright's two great passions: football and
show business.

home matches at Goodison Park, often accompanied by his partner, actress and
television star, Jenny Seagrove. It is thanks to Bill's initiative that the bronze statue
of the Toffees' all-time hero, Dixie Dean, now graces the entrance to Everton's
hallowed Goodison Park ground.

Any Dream Will Do, the television search for a new star for Joseph, had viewers
glued to their seats and their phones for weeks on end in 2007. Bill Kenwright CBE
proved himself totally at ease in front of the cameras as presenter/adjudicator. His
career seems to have come full-circle. What a joy it would be if Gordon Clegg, the
handsome young Corrie lad were to return as the now multi-millionaire mogul
metamorphosis of his alter-ego!

Carla Lane

Comedy Writer and Charity Champion

Carla spent her childhood and teenage years in West Derby, attended West Derby Village School and achieved the distinction of coming third from bottom of the class! She loved animals and thought it perfectly normal for her grandmother to have several monkeys swinging about from the airing rack, high up near the kitchen ceiling.

Recently, when asked if she has had any interesting jobs apart from her main career, she answered candidly, 'No. But several boring ones. I left school at fourteen and worked in a tiny local shop, called Daintyland, selling baby linen, knitting wools and sewing materials. Then I moved to the perfumery department at Bon Marché, later known as George Henry Lee's and now part of the John Lewis chain. I was promoted to window dresser because of the artistic way I displayed the items in the cosmetic cases. I married young and had two sons.' She continues, 'I'm lucky to be alive. At twenty-two I nearly died from meningitis.'

By the time her sons were at school and Carla was no longer going out to work, her creativity had blossomed and she began to think of writing, but she wasn't sure what. She had always written poetry and still does, but that wasn't enough. When she met fellow writer, Myra Taylor, they immediately sparked ideas together. They used to rendezvous at the Adelphi Hotel in the city centre, order coffee, sit for hours and bounce ideas off each other. Soon they had the embryo of a situation comedy, ready to pitch to the BBC. This was the era of the Mary Quant mini-skirt fashions. Carla and Myra made a strikingly attractive duo, both slim, one blonde wearing a black mini dress with white accessories, the other brunette, in white with black trimmings. Soft Courrèges boots drew attention to their long, slim legs. No wonder the 'powers that were' at the Beeb took one look and accepted *The Liver Birds* immediately. The series was an enormous success and ran for several years. As well as starring Nerys Hughes, Polly James and later Elizabeth Estensen, newcomer Julie Walters once had a tiny part and John Nettles started his career by appearing in a few episodes.

Flying solo, Carla went on to pen other hugely popular sitcoms. The romantic and delightfully scatty *Butterflies* made stars of Wendy Craig, Geoffrey Palmer and Nicholas Lyndhurst. *No Strings*, *The Mistress* and *I Woke Up One Morning* followed. Then the startling originality of *Bread* had audiences laughing from the opening shots to the final credits. The dysfunctional but eminently loveable Scouse family tickled the nation's funny bone, soon found its way into everybody's hearts and stayed there for series after series. Between 1980 and 1984, Carla won five different trophies for best comedy scripts.

A totally different award of which Carla is very proud is the top RSPCA award for her dedicated work on behalf of animals. While talking on the phone, she is surrounded by two dogs, eight tortoises, ten cats and thirteen parrots. When she lived in West Derby she owned a rare pedigree Chow dog. They made a handsome pair as they walked in the nearby Sandfield Park.

Carla's grandfather, a seafaring man was greatly disturbed by the fate of livestock being transported by ship. 'He discovered that in the hold, these poor creatures were herded together with no supports or divisions', says Carla. 'Consequently, the movement of the storm waves made them fall about and bang into each other. Very soon, they were injured and in pain and left to suffer for the rest of the voyage. My grandfather was so outraged he set about persuading the RSPCA to get the law changed to improve conditions for animals in transit. I'm following in his footsteps.'

Carla herself has campaigned vociferously (with a loudhailer) against poor travelling conditions for sheep en route to France. In recent years she bought an island reserve for wildlife and she cares for numerous animals in the grounds and stables of her enormous sixteenth-century home. To gain wider recognition for the needs of all creatures, Carla founded the charity Animaline, and turned her home into a rescue centre.

Although working so diligently for her friends in the animal kingdom, Carla has never sought the limelight for herself. Her talent is of the 'behind-the-scenes' kind. She is shy when appearing in public. Receiving awards has always been a mixed blessing for her. When she received one of her Best Scriptwriter Awards, she was mortified when the trophy fell through the bottom of the box before she could leave the stage. On another occasion, when Sir Lew Grade had only just completed his speech, Carla was so full of nerves, she walked off the stage before he had the chance to present her with her award. 'He had to trail behind me to my table and offer it to me there.' She cringes at the thought. Still in the realms of presentations, Carla recalls her most embarrassing experience ever. It occurred when the Queen honoured Carla with the OBE. 'I was so scared,' says Carla, 'as I left the chamber, I took a wrong turning. I followed a passageway, looking for something recognisable but it was all so confusing. I must have gone around in some sort of circle because suddenly I found myself in the worst kind of nightmare. I was wandering back across the stage in front of the Queen! The orchestra immediately changed its tune and played "Here We Go Again". Everyone in the room burst into laughter and applause and I was near to dying with embarrassment!'

Carla recalls the years when she was writing *Bread* and *Butterflies* as her salad days (she's a vegetarian). 'But the BBC changed completely and the young folk took over. Don't get me wrong – I like the young folk but I didn't like their scripts at that time. Although my sanctuary has grown and we are doing wonders for the animals, my once-upon-a-time wealth is on its last legs. When the BBC and all the other channels changed so radically, I couldn't seem to change the way I wrote. But I've got my second wind now and I'm ready to surprise everyone with two revolutionary new ideas. Watch this space.'

Canon Thomas Major Lester
1829–1903

Give the Child a Fair Chance

He was known as 'a Great Heart', 'Friend of the Friendless', and 'Friends of the Widow, Father Of The Orphan'. His epitaph was 'He was loved by all because he showed love to all'. His statue in St John's Gardens is twinned with that of his dear friend, Father Nugent (see p. 97). Quotations referring to Canon Major Lester, vicar of St Mary's Church, Honorary Canon of Liverpool and Rural Dean of Liverpool North, tell the story of a remarkable man, revered by all who knew him and remembered with great affection by all he helped.

Lester's family were originally from London. Initially he attended a private primary school as well as being tutored by his highly intelligent mother. At the age of ten, young Thomas travelled alone, up to Newcastle-under-Lyme, where he continued his education before studying at Christ's College, Cambridge, gaining his BA in 1852 and adding an MA in 1866.

Between these two dates, he married Jessie Madrell, the warm-hearted, intelligent niece of Sir Henry Madrell MP. During their married life, Thomas and Jessie Major Lester had ten children, five of whom died. Infant mortality was accepted as part of everyday existence in Liverpool at that time. In the poor areas it was often the parents who perished. This left starving, barefoot orphans to roam the streets in search of food and shelter.

Already dedicated to a life of devotion, prayer and philanthropy, their own tragic losses intensified the desire in the Major Lesters to rectify the problems they could see all around them in their Kirkdale Parish and beyond. The Revd Mr Major Lester, like his friend Father Nugent, took it upon himself to rescue as many as possible of these deprived and desolate waifs and strays. He would gather up any street urchins he found and persuade volunteers to help feed and clothe them. In the early days it was a struggle to finance this and much came out of his own pocket. But as he was noted for his excellent sermons, attendance at his morning and evening services were enthusiastic and regular. He began to receive donations to help his good causes. When he decided he must do even more to lift these tragic little creatures out of their pitiful existence, he raised more funds by writing personally to local dignitaries and to the newspapers. This personal approach was appreciated by the business community and a response was always forthcoming.

His charitable efforts started in a humble way. In fact the first school for the very poorest infants started its existence over a coal shed in Walton Road. Members of his congregation and beyond were so impressed by his earnest and moving sermons, they were eager to help in a variety of ways. One Sunday morning, a wealthy parishioner was so inspired, she wished she could hear exactly the same sermon again. She offered the preacher the handsome amount of £5 if he would repeat his address, word for word, that evening. Much as he would have liked to use this extremely generous donation, he refused to bore his congregation, instead taking a different text at evensong and recounting different stories.

Another lady, however, found an acceptable way of benefiting Lester's Kirkdale Child Charity. She often visited the home personally and, to commemorate the premature death of her own son, she donated over a hundred items of his clothing. To these she later added another hundred of her own. Mrs Cliff, who owned a large house and grounds, Claremont in West Derby, continued to benefit the cause by inviting teachers from the Ragged Schools to join her for meals at her own home, surrounded as it was by open countryside. This house was later owned by Carla Lane.

In spite of their dire circumstances, some Liverpool orphans were reluctant to try to better themselves. They could see no point in learning to read, write and acquire useful skills. To tempt them, Thomas Major Lester would offer free breakfast, lunch and tea between lessons, all with tasty ingredients. It never failed. As well as the basics, Thomas also persuaded musicians to coach pupils at his refuge for boys and girls. Various bands were formed and these often went out on parade in the streets, a welcome sound in the days before radio and gramophone. Funds for the schools and homes were collected when the bands were engaged at festivals and celebrations.

At the home, Thomas sensitively banned any signs of charity or condescension. As well as receiving a sound education, children were housed in warm, comfortable surroundings and never made to feel that they were a burden. There were concerts, parties, sports days and treats. Every summer the children were taken across the Mersey by ferry, for picnics and games in the woods and fields at Eastham.

The canon (as he was from 1884 onwards) made sure there was no discrimination between the sexes. To him, all classes, nationalities, creeds and genders were equal in the sight of the Lord. Boys were apprenticed to various trades, especially tailoring and printing, and at their 'passing out' ceremonies there would be a banquet of roast geese, plum pudding and cakes, with a presentation of books to mark good conduct and punctuality. Likewise, girls learned knitting, sewing, lace-making, cookery and dressmaking.

Local families were also drawn into Canon Lester's perceptive benevolence. Owing to the short life expectancy of the time, there were many widows left with young families but with no financial support of any kind, who needed to go out to work. The homes took in toddlers on a temporary basis, freeing the mothers to find employment. Conversely, widows without children were encouraged to take in the teenage orphans after they had finished their tuition and apprenticeship.

At the canon's funeral in 1903, the music was provided by Father Nugent's Boys' Band and the streets were lined by an enormous crowd. Father Nugent's tribute was, 'Canon Lester and I, with the Revd Canon Postance and Revd Stowell Brown were among the originators of the Hot Pot Fund and I have not found three dearer friends. We all had the idea of trying to reduce crime by attending to the neglected children. In Canon Lester there was no narrowness. His hand was ever open. His heart sympathised with the poor of every denomination.'

William Hesketh Lever 1851–1925

Lord Leverhulme – Businessman and Philanthropist

If, by chance, you have never visited Port Sunlight Village, please do take a day trip there soon. It's not far from Liverpool. You can get there by rail, by car through the Mersey Tunnels or by ferry across the Mersey and onward by bus. Stroll around its beautifully laid out avenues, bordered by formal rosebeds and lawns. Wander through the gardens of the landscaped park, over the little rustic bridge where so many brides love to be photographed. Pause at the monumental cenotaph to honour the names of the fallen in two world wars. Admire the overall sense of uniformity in the architecture of the 'desirable residences', but look long enough to realise that within this general style, there is plenty of scope for individuality. No boring lines of identical terraced houses but wide, curving approaches to either the church, the village hall, the bowling green, the inn, the Gladstone Theatre or to the factory discreetly tucked away in one corner of the village.

Last but not least, walk up the steps of the imposing classical-style art gallery. Once inside, admire the masterly oil paintings, pieces of splendid antique furniture and collections of fine porcelain from around the world. Rest for a while and take some refreshment in the oak-panelled tea rooms.

While you do so, reflect upon the life and work of the remarkable man whose visionary innovation brought all this into being, in a region where once there was nothing but acres of marshy wasteland.

And for what reason was it all built? For an idyllic sanctuary for the rich and privileged? For a folly, without real purpose, just to gratify the whim of an eccentric millionaire? No. These comfortable homes in their picturesque and airy setting were created for factory workers. Men and women of the previously barren surroundings who would otherwise have been unemployed and poverty-stricken. At one time there were just no jobs in this area, no houses, no recreational facilities, no community of any sort.

Until, that is, the seventh child of Mr and Mrs James Lever finally put in an appearance, after Eliza Lever had tried and failed six times to produce a son and heir, instead of the sextet of girls who preceded him. William Hesketh Lever, as he was christened, eventually had three other siblings, only one of whom was another boy, James Darcy Lever.

Let me take you back to the year 1851. This was the year of William's much longed-for birth. Picture Victorian England in the North-West. Narrow, straight streets, smoke-blackened brickwork, windows smeared by smog and frost, front doors that opening directly onto the road, often without even a protective strip of pavement. Or the bleak countryside where farmers laboured to eke out a meagre living. In spite of this, William's childhood was reasonably secure, as his father had worked his way up in a prospering grocery business in Bolton. Because he was the long-awaited, first-born son, William was immediately treated as someone very special. Everything pointed to his importance in the family and he soon developed a supremely confident personality. Furthermore, he instinctively knew that he had forward-thinking and innovative ideas, far ahead of the conventions of his time. His character was also very affectionate and caring. His loyalty to family and friends were to last all his life.

Indeed, his little chum Jonathan Simpson, from the infant school across the road from William's home, became his life-long friend, colleague and confidante. In the same school, a pretty little girl, Elizabeth Hulme, caught William's eye, soon became his childhood sweetheart and years later, after their marriage, never left his side. She was his tower of strength, his travelling companion and a warm and competent hostess to his many business and titled acquaintances. Their love and respect for each other was unwavering.

William was brought up following the Non-conformist faith, with its belief in hard work, service to others, physical fitness, self-discipline and in using one's waking hours to good purpose. Indeed, in the whole of William's life, there was never a moment of idleness nor self-indulgence. Always up at the crack of dawn, into a cold shower, he was constantly looking for new ventures, improvements to working conditions and fresh fields to colonise.

During his apprenticeship in his father's shop, William's job included slicing up huge bars of soap into manageable sizes for customers to carry away. He also had to break up the large slabs of sugar and cut them into cubes. He soon realised that it was preferable to deal with the sugar first before moving on to the soap. His hands might be clean after the soap but the sugar might not taste very palatable! The sugar came from Henry Tate's business. The Tate who made generous donations to Liverpool University and gave his name to the highly acclaimed art galleries, one of which now stands at the Albert Dock complex, on Liverpool's waterfront.

After William's youngest brother Darcy joined the business, William turned his attention to the finances and accounts of the shop. He soon reorganised this to make it more efficient and thus more profitable. He then persuaded his father to buy him a pony and trap and let him go out as a sales rep, drumming up far more orders than his father had ever hoped for.

The energetic William had the wanderlust and soon found a valid reason to travel to Ireland and to France in search of good quality, low-priced farm produce. At home, he made sure that the name Lever spread beyond his home town of Bolton, to Wigan and then to Liverpool. Back at the main premises, William and

Darcy worked together to devise more efficient protective packaging for the imported eggs. They also created a thriving demand for their Irish butter. By this time, Jonathan Simpson had qualified as an architect and the boyhood pals teamed up to plan improved headquarters for the business.

In about 1884, William decided to concentrate on one special aspect of the Lever sales. He favoured the soap. He even thought that instead of paying another firm to manufacture it, Levers could purchase the ingredients and make it themselves. The novelty way to market it would be to pre-wrap the small bars to appeal to female customers in particular. Ahead of his time, as always, he realised that subliminal persuasion could influence choice. He registered the soap under the trade name of 'Sunlight'. What more could anyone desire?

He even invented more refined recipes to add to the varieties on offer. Then he instituted a campaign of direct advertising, employing top quality artists to design bright, cheerful posters, metal plaques and magazine advertisements. The business flourished and Port Sunlight Village, between Liverpool and Chester was founded. The idea being that a wholesome environment would promote contentment and increased efficiency. The standard of living for the Lever workforce was far above the norm for that era. As productivity increased, further stages of development were added to the village. Employees travelled in from Liverpool to supplement local labour. Some settled and took up permanent residence.

William and Elizabeth made frequent visits to Liverpool to the theatre, for parties, social occasions and often to the law courts, due to William's various vigorous legal battles with rivals and suppliers.

William was reluctantly persuaded to stand for Parliament but he soon found the tedious machinations of government too frustrating for his go-getting personality. He liked to formulate a plan and see his vision come to fruition all within a given timescale. Endless debates and delays were not his scene at all. He cut short his political career and concentrated on what he did best, making soap and making his workers happy.

Still working with his brother (although Darcy's health was nowhere near as robust as William's) Lever's expanded into other products such as Mac Fisheries and palm oil. He travelled the world in search of new ingredients. He even attempted to become a benefactor in the Western Isles of Scotland but sadly was not able to repeat the success of his Port Sunlight Village. He was, however, honoured in 1917, by being raised to the peerage and he took his seat in the House of Lords. He chose to extend his surname by adding his darling wife's maiden name to his own. So he became Lord Leverhulme. He also showed his love and devotion to Elizabeth by naming the beautiful Port Sunlight Museum the Lady Lever Art Gallery. Such was the amazing reputation of the village, that King George V and Queen Mary paid a visit and were escorted around by Lord Leverhulme and the quietly confident, stylishly attired Lady Lever, at heart still the sweet little girl from Miss Aspinall's primary school in Bolton. Their Majesties were then royally entertained at Thornton Manor on the Wirral Peninsula, the country seat of the Lever family.

Stylish architecture typifies the picturesque originality of the purpose-built workers' homes in Port Sunlight Village, Wirral.

After William's death, the factory prospered well into the twentieth century. Even though the factory no longer makes soap, the neighbouring Gladstone Theatre constantly hosts plays, concerts and shows of an extremely high standard, by both local and professional companies. Such is the domestic quality of the housing, now that residence is no longer restricted to employees of the factory, the neighbourhood is what vendors describe as a 'much sought-after area'. And the beautiful art gallery, administered by the Art Galleries and Museums of Merseyside still displays collections to match any in the land. It has even been featured in television and cinema films to typify all that is best in elegant architecture. What a legacy for the people of Merseyside and Wirral

Gerry Marsden

Gerry and the Pacemakers

On 19 October 1961, the audience at Litherland Town Hall, Halton Hill Road, Liverpool, must surely have been the most privileged pop fans of all time. This unique occasion beats all other concerts, worldwide. Forget the Hollywood Bowl, the Far East, Hamburg, the Cavern and any football stadium anywhere. No. Litherland Town Hall is the only venue to have hosted an evening with the pop group, The Beatmakers. Who? No, not The Who, The Beatmakers.

The line-up consisted of Gerry Marsden, Freddie Marsden, 'Dixie' Dean, Jim Tobin, George Harrison, John Lennon, Paul McCartney and Ringo Starr. Get it? Under the aegis of Brian Epstein's management, both groups joined together for this one and only gig. Some gig, eh?

At the other end of Liverpool, Gerry and his older brother, Freddie were born in Dingle. Both attended Our Lady of Mount Carmel School in North Hill Street and Gerry sang in the church choir. Their father was a railway clerk and enjoyed playing the ukulele and the drums. Like Gerry, he was a talented handyman around the house. For young Freddie, their Dad once made an improvised drum by stretching an old drumskin over an empty tin of Quality Street.

When teenage Gerry and Freddie joined forces with Jim Tobin and 'Dixie' Dean to form a skiffle group, the 'double bass' was constructed from a wooden tea chest with musical strings skilfully attached to it. It is probably no coincidence that one of Gerry's first jobs after leaving school was that of a tea-chest maker for Kardomah. The Kardomah tearooms were very popular meeting places in Liverpool city centre.

Apart from youth boxing, Gerry's interest was lighthearted music, singing, playing and composing. As well as guitar, he enjoyed the piano and the alto sax. After a while, the skiffle group was transformed into a pop group. Using the first part of their surname and because they were playing bars of music, Mars Bars seemed an ideal name. Mr Marsden approached the manufacturers but they refused permission to use the name. What a lost opportunity for fantastic publicity. Are they kicking themselves now? Gerry bounced back. Hearing a sports commentator talking about heart pacemakers gave him the inspiration for the equally brilliant name which brought them worldwide fame.

The group drove themselves to Hamburg and played in the Top Ten club. Their hours were long and exhausting. The smoky atmosphere, amplified music and prolonged singing had an effect on Gerry's voice. His pleasantly husky tone owes its origins to Hamburg. On their return from Germany, the Pacemakers alternated with the Beatles at lunchtime sessions in the Cavern. It was there that Brian Epstein discovered them. He signed them and began to promote their image as the easy-going boys-next-door type. The Litherland Town Hall gig was one of their earliest engagements with him.

A great opportunity presented itself after The Beatles chose not to record 'How Do You Do It?' The number was offered to Gerry and co. It immediately soared to number one in the charts. This was closely followed by their next two singles, 'I Like It' and 'You'll Never Walk Alone'. They set a record for a new group having three consecutive number ones with their three debut singles. Their future was assured, and more bouncy, catchy tunes followed.

When Tony Warren, the creator of *Coronation Street*, wrote a film script especially for them, featuring fascinating glimpses of Merseyside, they hit a new high. America, China and Italy had all been subjects of songs before but now Gerry gave the world 'Ferry 'Cross The Mersey'. It became an instant hit and all-time favourite.

Gerry had always liked the musical *Carousel*, particularly the emotive song 'You'll Never Walk Alone'. His choice had enormous impact on fans everywhere. Liverpool Football Club took it up as their anthem and it is still sung with fantastic fervour at all the Reds' matches today. Gerry sometimes attends matches and delights thousands by joining in.

After The Pacemakers went their separate ways, Gerry starred in the West End musical *Charlie Girl*. Meeting the Queen was a special moment for Gerry, when he received his MBE. No doubt she spoke not only of his music but also of the many charities he supports. Only recently, in conjunction with Travelwise, Gerry went striding out with a group of children who will never walk alone if they all take a little exercise. He is encouraging them to save money, cut down on pollution, boost their health and make new friends too, as they walk to school instead of taking the bus.

It isn't only Scousers at the Kop who think the world of Gerry and his music. Our cousins down under can't get enough of him, either. The Aussies invite him back time after time and he has toured the Antipodes for the last twenty-three years. He loves it there and they love him. 'Don't Let The Sun Catch You Crying', was an enormous hit for Gerry. When he is in Australia or New Zealand, no one is likely to see him crying.

Gerry considers himself to be a fortunate man. He is rarely seen without a smile on his face. A happy marriage to Pauline and a secure family life with his two daughters, Yvette-Louise and Victoria-Ann, are the basis of this. He is content to keep his private life private and never gives the gossip columnists any inspiration. When asked about the best period of his life, his serene reply is: 'From 1963 until I die!'

Sharon Maughan
'Instant' Success for Beautiful Actress

The date: sometime in the 1980s; the time: evening; the place: your lounge; action: you are relaxing on the sofa after your evening meal, ready to put your feet up and watch your favourite programme on the box. But before the main feature begins, here is something everyone loves, the commercial for Nescafé Gold Blend coffee.

Ever since the very first episode of this cult series of television adverts, audiences all over Britain have been glued to their seats. Such is the charismatic appeal of the two immensely attractive young people on screen that the moment the background music begins, everything else is forgotten and the next thirty seconds become more important than the sum of the other three hours that follow.

The shy, tentative meeting between the newcomer and the already resident flat-dweller, the gradual realisation of that certain '*je ne sais quoi*', 'allure', 'magnetism' – call it what you like – the imagined aroma of the fresh coffee and the eventual passionate romance between these young lovers, repeated many times during nearly a decade, was something everyone wanted to share. Sales of instant coffee rocketed, sparking off the fashion for coffee bars and cafés still in vogue today.

For Sharon Mughan (as she spelled her name then) and Anthony Head, later the star of *Buffy the Vampire Slayer* and *Little Britain*, it meant immediate stardom for both and the assurance of long and successful careers to come.

So, who was this enigmatic and cultured young actress? Someone from the Home Counties, educated at boarding school and a finishing school in Paris? Daughter of a wealthy professional family?

Let Sharon tell you her story in her own words, 'I was born in Westvale, Kirkby, Liverpool. I went to St Gregory's Comprehensive School for Girls. Times were very hard and money in extremely short supply. I sometimes can't believe how lucky I was to live during the time of Harold Wilson's government. If it wasn't for him, neither myself nor my brothers would have been able to continue our education. We each got full grants and that was the beginning of the rest of my life.'

Until the age of fourteen, Sharon had never been on holiday, had never ridden in a car and her mother could not even afford to buy Sharon's school photo. Sharon would dearly have loved to take piano lessons but a piano was way beyond their means.

'When I left school,' Sharon continues, 'I wanted to go to RADA to earn some money. I worked all through the summer at the Kraft cheese factory. They thought it took three weeks to train anyone to pack Dairylea cheese spread quarters into the little round boxes. I quickly got so good (and so bored) that I started to take my book to read while I was doing it. But not for long! They confiscated my copy of *Catcher In The Rye*, and for the next ten weeks I was condemned to watching the wheel go round and round. I was on shift work. Six in the morning until midday, or two until ten. On the early shift, in order to 'clock in' on time, I had to take two buses, starting at 4.30 a.m., then changing to a second route by 5.30 a.m. I still think of those days and I'd like to pass on my best wishes and good luck to anyone still doing it.'

After leaving RADA, Sharon's first role was as Ophelia, the delicate and tragic love interest in Shakespeare's *Hamlet*. Then came the television series *Shabby Tiger*, a host of individual appearances and then the coffee adverts. When Sharon was later cast in an episode of *Morse* with John Thaw, she had to utter the line, 'Coffee! Ugh, I hate coffee. It gives me a headache!'

Sharon has also appeared in productions of *The Enigma Files*, *The Flame Trees of Thika*, *A Doll's House*, *Arcadia*, *Another Stake Out* and *Nice Guy Eddie*, set in Liverpool and starring Ricky Tomlinson. In *Heartbeat*, she played Ursula Dean who, rejected by Lord Ashfordly, returns to wreak her revenge upon him.

The favourite period in Sharon's career came, in the recent years, when she played Tricia Williams in eighty episodes of *Holby City*. Researching for this role, she spent time at Watford General Hospital learning correct nursing procedures and getting to know real patients. 'I loved everyone at *Holby City*,' she emphasises, 'they were all wonderful to work with.'

Sharon has been happily married to actor Trevor Eve since 1980. They have two sons and a daughter, Alice Eve, who is now a successful actress in her own right.

Currently, Sharon has embarked upon a fresh venture. She runs her own thriving film company where she divides her time between writing, directing and producing. This busy lady continues to act as well. A new film, released in 2008, *The Bank Job*, stars Jason Statham, Saffron Burrows and Sharon Maughan as Sonia Bern. She can now afford any piano she fancies.

She says she would like more involvement with breast cancer charities. 'I'm negotiating with them at the moment,' she says, 'and I'd also like more involvement with Liverpool.'

In conclusion, Sharon pays tribute to her Mum, Nora Mughan, 'Who scrubbed other people's floors so that I could have my dream.'

Sir Paul McCartney

Yesterday, Today and all Our Tomorrows – the Ongoing Story

There can hardly be a person in the civilised world who has not heard of The Beatles. Their music has became an intrinsic part of everyday life and any Merseysider holidaying abroad has only to mention the word 'Liverpool' to be greeted immediately with a broad smile and the response, 'Ahh! Beatles!'

Before a chance meeting with George Harrison on a bus, Paul McCartney had attended Stockton Wood Infant School in Speke, then Joseph Williams Junior School in Belle Vale. At the age of eleven, Paul was one of only four boys to pass the entrance exam to attend the Liverpool Institute Grammar School for Boys.

As a teenager, after meeting John Lennon and forming a pop group including George Harrison and Stuart Sutcliffe, called The Quarrymen, Paul and John began to write their own music and lyrics. Eventually, after Stuart's tragically sudden death, there were replacements first by Pete Best, then Ringo Starr. Gigs in Hamburg and regular lunchtime concerts at the Cavern in Liverpool city centre brought them to the notice of Brian Epstein. He became their self-appointed manager/agent/entrepreneur, and began to introduce them to the main record companies in London. With a change of image and a change of name to The Beatles, Britain and America went crazy with what became known as Beatlemania. Such a wild phenomenon had never before been experienced. Their compositions were, and still are, played everywhere and all the time, right into the twenty-first century.

The song 'Yesterday', composed and performed entirely by Paul McCartney, backed by a string instrumental group, not The Beatles, is one of the most popular pieces ever performed in the history of music. Numerous artists have included it in their repertoires and it is said that at any given moment, 'Yesterday' is being played somewhere in the world.

After the break-up of The Beatles, Paul formed his own group, Wings, introducing his wife, Linda, as one of the performers. Theirs was an exceptionally happy marriage, with a close-knit family, one of whom, Stella, is now a famous fashion designer. Since Linda's devastatingly young death, Paul has lovingly kept her memory alive in a variety of ways, all to the benefit of others. He has played in memorial charity concerts, continued her support for animal charities, promoted her belief in the principles of vegetarianism and endowed two very special souvenirs in her name. Both continue to be of enormous benefit to subsequent generations of Liverpudlians. Firstly, in the beautifully landscaped Calderstones Park, there is now the Linda McCartney Play Area for young children. This is always full of kiddies having a fantastic time on the swings, slides and huge climbing net. It has safety ground cover and occupies a sunny spot near the vast playing field and the majestic, mature trees of the park. Secondly, and probably even more importantly, at the Royal Liverpool University Hospital, doctors and staff at the Linda McCartney Clinic continue their

Macca swings high at the Linda McCartney
Play Area in Calderstones Park

Students rehearse on the 'stone suitcases' sculpture
outside the Liverpool Institute for the Performing Arts.

nestimable and highly appreciated screening, diagnosis and protection of women's
health. The heartfelt gratitude of patients and their families cannot be overestimated.

Sir Paul also has a deep regard for the cultural side of Liverpool life. Long before
the city's Capital of Culture year, Paul secured the future of his old school's building. It
had originally been designed as a Mechanics' Institute in 1837 but, by 1980, no longer
needed as a school of any sort, the building was scheduled to be demolished. However,
by 1996, thanks to Sir Paul's generosity and foresight, it had been transformed into
the Liverpool Institute for the Performing Arts, known universally as LIPA. Behind its
imposing façade, Sir Paul funded and supervised an amazing metamorphosis,
revamping the interior and installing world-class facilities. Breathing new life into this
phoenix-like academy, he has created superb training opportunities for people not
only from the North-West but also from further afield. The guiding ethos is to equip
students with wide-ranging qualifications in every aspect of the performing arts.

Music, dance, theatre and technical expertise all feature in LIPA's diploma,
degree and post-graduate courses. On Saturdays, its doors are also open to children
aged from four to nineteen. Its impressive frontage on Mount Street adjoins with
Hope Street and the cultural heart of the city. It is just around the corner from the
art college, close to the Royal Liverpool Philharmonic Hall, the Everyman Theatre,
both cathedrals, the Medical Institution and the uniquely beautiful Chinese Arch.
No better site could possibly be found to help budding thespians immerse
themselves in artistic surroundings.

It was said of Sir Christopher Wren, architect of St Paul's Cathedral, 'if you want a
memorial of him, look around you.' In Liverpool, the same is true of Sir Paul
McCartney. Universally, you can hear him anywhere, any time. 'All You Need Is Love'.

Jimmy McGovern
The Whole Truth

Ordinary people. People who think they have an ordinary life and are living it their way. Suddenly they are caught up in a catastrophe, a crisis beyond their control. They want justice. They want their story told to the world. Some turn to the national press and other media. More and more turn to one man. A man whose voice is heard, whose work is respected on more than one level and who makes a lasting impact on the conscience and consciousness of the nation – Jimmy McGovern.

Before Jimmy became a writer, he had a wide experience in a variety of jobs, working on a production line in a car factory, then in a chemical works At one time he was a bus conductor, at another the manager of a betting shop and then a school

teacher at Calderstones Comprehensive School. These all brought him into contact with many different personalities and many walks of life. As well as integrity, empathy and sympathy are probably the two key features of his psyche and he uses them to the full in his efforts on behalf of his fellow men and women.

As a youngster, Jimmy attended both the primary and grammar sections of St Francis Xaviour school. He was one of a family of nine, whose parents had only limited means. Opportunities for improvement were few and far between. While he was still a teenager, he married and soon had two children to support.

His earliest foray into the literary world came in the years between 1981 and 1990, via scriptwriting for the Liverpool-based soap opera *Brookside*, created by Phil Redmond. The innovative approach here, in which the usual romantic themes were interwoven with stronger topics such as strikes, rape, a domestic siege, lesbianism, incest and murder appealed to Jimmy's talent for drama in everyday settings. In 1994, Jimmy's detective series, *Cracker*, proved an instant success and brought him his first BAFTA award, followed by his controversial film *Priest*, and later, *The Lakes*.

After the disaster at Hillsborough, with the devastating loss of life of young football fans, Jimmy was approached on his own doorstep by two heartbroken mothers who had lost their children at the scene. Knowing his ability, they begged him to investigate and report the truth of the disaster. To ensure accuracy and fairness, Jimmy met many bereaved families and researched every detail, even enlisting experienced colleagues to verify his findings. The effect of the programme was so challenging and so moving that more awards and another BAFTA came his way. But Jimmy felt strongly that the dignity shown by the mourning relatives also deserved recognition and he was concerned that they were not able to share the honours.

He describes the time that he spent with the sacked Liverpool dockers in 1977, when he was working on a drama about their industrial dispute, as 'a joy'. He respected the men so much, that he decided he wanted no monetary reward for this script. So his entire fee for his eighteen months' fact-finding went into the dockers' funds and by involving the workers themselves in the writing, he knew that he, as an individual, would not be eligible for any awards.

Sunday, the powerful account of Bloody Sunday in Northern Ireland, was written at the invitation of Gaslight Productions. It took a great deal of persuasion before Jimmy at last agreed to become involved in the revisiting of this historical disaster from more than thirty years ago. As with his previous docu-dramas, before he wrote a word, he went right to the source of the situation. With help from his colleague, Katy Jones, an experienced television producer from *World In Action*, over 150 of the people involved in both sides of the debacle were interviewed. Once again, the result was a compelling and thought-provoking drama that created a lasting impression on the viewing public.

In 2007, Jimmy's series called *The Street*, dealing with the emotional relationships within a group of fictional families all living in the same northern town road, won him another BAFTA. It was so well-received that a second, even more dynamic series, was commissioned and transmitted within the same twelve months.

Yet another request, this time from a man he met in his local pub in Kensington, Liverpool, was the starting point for Jimmy's venture into the field of theatre. Ian Brownbill, a brass band enthusiast, who aims to transform Liverpool's Edge Hill station into a major new arts centre, suggested the true story of how the blockade of the cotton ports, during the American Civil War, caused repercussions for the workers in the Lancashire cotton mills. Jimmy developed the idea into a heart-rending drama concerning the black slaves on the western side of the Atlantic and the desperately poor white mill workers on the British side. Both groups suffered under appalling conditions and brutish masters. Powerful music, beautifully performed, adds to the atmosphere; music derived on the one hand from negro spirituals, on the other from the famous brass bands of the northern mill towns. The show, superbly brought to life by the nationally celebrated director, Liverpool's own Jude Kelly, played to packed audiences at the Salford Lowry Theatre and at the Liverpool Empire Theatre in 2007.

Jimmy has a special regard for the Lyndale Cancer Care Day Centre in Knowsley, which provides leisure and relaxation activities, refreshments, friendly company and emotional support for anyone undergoing treatment.

When asked about the highlights of his career, Jimmy says, 'There are no real highlights. I've enjoyed it all.' He adds, 'I'm lucky to have won most of the awards on offer in this country.'

Many people would say that luck has nothing to do with it. Dedicated hard work and utter integrity, more like!

George Melly 1926–2007
Good Time George – The Dean of Decadence

Larger than life in every sense, George Melly, the jazz musician, was multi-talented, highly intelligent, a skilled fisherman, full of fun and fond of the low life. One of Liverpool's most ebullient sons, George Melly was born in the Aigburth area and went to Parkfield School. As a young child he was fascinated by the Punch and Judy shows created and performed by the man who called himself Professor Codman. Although usually associated with seaside promenades, these weird puppets in their red-and-white-striped booth and bizarre clothes often enacted their violent quarrels in St John's Lane, at the side of St George's Hall, near the centre of Liverpool. George never forgot their anarchy nor their flamboyant style of dress.

He and his sister, the actress Andrée Melly, grew up in a comfortable middle-class home. They were descended on their mother's side from Jewish grandparents and on the paternal side from Swiss ancestors. Their mother adored anything to do with the theatre, the ballet and films, with a preference for comedies. She loved to mix with visiting stars Michael Redgrave, Robert Helpman and Frederick Ashton. It must have been from her that George inherited his genius for clowning. As an adult his extravagantly mimed interpretations of jazz songs became integral to his act. In such numbers as 'Frankie and Johnny', he would accompany the lyrics with suitable actions for both the sex and the murder involved. He loved to shock his audiences with lewd facial expressions and suggestive body language. His idol was the American blues singer, Bessie Smith. He copied her style and sang many of her songs.

George's main education was as a boarder at the prestigious public school, Stowe, where creativity was encouraged and prominence given to all the arts as well as to academic excellence. This suited George's wide-ranging talents, as did its motto 'I stand firm. I stand first'.

In his professional life his musical talents took him into jazz cellars and clubs all around Britain, most notably Ronnie Scott's, as well as the club owned by Johnny Dankworth and Cleo Laine. These associations were successful during at least three decades. He was also extremely popular at university student union celebrations around the country. In fact, his own wild, student-like behaviour was something of which he was inordinately proud.

In his four superbly entertaining autobiographies, he boasted about his rollicking days and nights of drinking, smoking, bisexual love affairs, two marriages, four children and general debauchery. More than any other boy, George could outdo rock groups, film stars and medieval monarchs in the outrageous behaviour department. His clothes were always ostentatious. His wide-brimmed fedora hats and, latterly, his eye-patch, were his trade mark. Self-indulgence he did with panache. 'Camp' and 'excessive' were two of his favourite words.

But as well as the raucous public figure, there was a surprisingly private side to his character. Who would imagine such an extrovert would find solace in the solitary sport of fly-fishing? Hours alone on the river bank were a great pleasure to him and he chose country homes to suit this lifestyle rather than living near the Soho clubs. He became such an expert that he wrote several books on fishing. Indeed, his writing talents easily matched his musical ability. At various times he took up the post of film critic, television critic and pop critic on the *Observer* newspaper. At the *Daily Mail*, he provided the words and often the ideas for Wally Fawkes's furry little cartoon character, 'Flook'. At *The Times* he teamed up with cartoonist Marc. He also wrote two film scripts, one of which starred Lynne Redgrave and Liverpool-born Rita Tushingham as two girls who leave the North to seek fun and adventure in swinging London. As the theme tune was *Georgie Girl*, maybe George drew on some of his own early aspirations.

Yet another aspect of this multi-faceted bohemian was his gift for painting and his love of the Surrealist movement in art. On Merseyside his Cubist-style painting of the beautifully restored Victorian Palm House at Sefton Park is much admired. At the end of the Second World War, after being demobbed from national service, Melly worked at a private art gallery in London and began to build up his own collection of Surrealist art and eventually became an authority on art in general. In 1997, the huge Walker Art Gallery in Liverpool invited him to open their season of Aubrey Beardsley's highly erotic illustrations from the very naughty 1920s. As virtually all of Beardsley's work was in monochrome, all guests were invited to dress entirely in black and white. Everyone did and while most paid homage to Beardsley, some ladies wore stylish trouser suits and fedoras in honour of Melly.

Time did nothing to diminish his irreverent lust for life, although the vulgarity was somewhat curtailed. In spite of seriously failing health, the early stages of dementia, poor eyesight and hearing problems, he never retired. Less than a month before his death at the age of eighty-one, he performed at a concert in aid of the dementia charity, Admiral Nurses. In spite of everything, his second, unconventional marriage lasted forty years to the end of his life.

When the show business newspaper, *The Stage*, tentatively asked him what he would like mentioned in a potential obituary, his characteristic reply was 'Nothing! Absolutely nothing, I'm far too busy!'

John Middleton 1578–1623

The Childe of Hale

How many times do young children ask, 'do you believe in . . . ?' Generally the answer is, 'No, they only exist in stories. There's no such thing as . . .' But when the question refers to giants, the answer should be a definite 'Yes'.

As the aeroplanes come in to land at the modern John Lennon Airport, they are descending ever nearer to the thatched rooftops of several elegant and highly desirable cottages in Hale Village, on the outskirts of Liverpool. Only a little closer to the rural backwaters of the River Mersey and the Hale Lighthouse, stands the church of St Mary's. In the cemetery there is a grave bearing the inscription, 'Here lyeth the bodie of John Middleton, nine foot three'.

Across the road, the local pub is called the Childe Of Hale. On a nearby pathway, there stands a totem pole-style carving representing the legendary figure of this area's most renowned inhabitant, while in Speke Hall and in Brasenose College, Oxford, there are portraits of this extraordinary personage. Even Samuel Pepys, the famous diarist makes mention of his abnormal size.

As all good fairytales begin, let us start like this . . . Once upon a time, in the year 1578, on the outskirts of Liverpool, a baby boy was born to humble peasant farmers. While he was still young he used to love watching the many different birds along the sandy shores of the nearby river. There was a cave which was his own favourite hiding place and, on the beach, he would sometimes draw a rough sketch of a giant and lie down inside its outline.

When he reached adolescence, he grew much more rapidly than the other teenagers in the village. Soon he was taller than his parents and easily dwarfed even the biggest and strongest men for miles around. He had to sleep with his feet sticking out of the bedroom window. The hook where he hung his coat was 10ft from the floor level and he could only stand upright in the very centre of his home, where the roof reached its highest point. He could no longer fit into his cave and he was now as big as the giant in the sand.

By the time he was an adult, he was acknowledged to be the tallest man in the world. His hands and feet were huge, his nose and lips were large and coarse-looking. There were gaps between his teeth, his skin was thick and oily and his voice was deep and gruff, and he was not likely to have any children.

The local squire, Gilbert Ireland, Lord of the Manor of Hale, decided that the towering John Middleton would make an ideal bodyguard. So he took him into his household. John was no longer a farm labourer for his father. He now accompanied his master everywhere, keeping out riff-raff and performing feats of strength to entertain the gentry after mealtimes. He was, to all intents and purposes, the medieval equivalent of a bouncer, a stunt-man and a Mr Universe all rolled into one.

The king at that time was James I. One day, on his way from Scotland to London, he made a visit to Liverpool, to confer a knighthood upon Gilbert Ireland.

King James believed in the supernatural and when he saw Middleton he was delighted to see confirmation of his notion that strange creatures really did exist. His Majesty invited the newly honoured Sir Gilbert and his colossal companion to visit him in London.

The people of Hale realised that their most famous resident couldn't turn up at court in his rough and ragged peasant clothing. In those days there was no question of popping down to Marks & Spencers on the nearby motorway. In any case M&S don't stock outsize tabards and hose. So the villagers and local dignitaries clubbed together and found a tailor who could rival any designer in the North. The resulting outfit was decorated with large ruffs at the neck and hands, a striped doublet of crimson and white, a blue girdle embroidered with gold, a matching belt, also blue and gold with a gold fringe, white breeches with blue flowers, green stockings and shoes with red heels and red ribbon bows. Looking like a walking rainbow was not thought to be over the top in those days! This Goliath of a Scouser, who could easily have inspired the tale of *Jack and the Beanstalk*, was quite happy to travel through Merseyside dressed up like a pantomime dame.

When he was presented at court, the monarch commanded him to wrestle with the king's own champion who was, himself, of great strength and huge proportion. All the noble sports fans of the time were assembled to watch the spectacle and there was much betting, with wagers of large sums of money. Just who was the actual winner is not clear but maybe the exhibition wasn't as spectacular as the king had been hoping. In any event, Middleton was not engaged for any further bouts but was sent away with the bountiful prize of 20 sovereigns, enough to keep him and his family in luxury for many years.

On the way home, Sir Gilbert made a stop at Oxford, to visit his alma mater of Brasenose College where he had been a student in 1578. He wanted to show off his immense trophy of a servant. While they were there, a tracing to illustrate the enormous size of Middleton's hand was outlined. This connection with Sir Gilbert Ireland is the reason why the life-sized portrait of the Childe of Hale was donated to Brasenose by Colonel Ireland Blackburne in 1924.

On Middleton's return journey to Hale, Sir Gilbert must have been elsewhere. If he had accompanied the Childe, the master might have prevented the servant from being duped and mugged. As it was, the giant arrived home with nothing to show for his 'fifteen minutes of fame'. The poor man had to return to ploughing the fields for the rest of his life.

So why should we believe a story that for many years was only an oral tradition, maybe a myth or even pure fiction? For two reasons. Firstly, in 1887, historians dug up some of Middleton's bones and measured them before returning them to their rightful resting place. Secondly, modern medicine chronicles very clearly the characteristics of the syndrome known as acromegaly. This is caused by a small, benign tumour in the pituitary gland which is situated in the centre of the skull, below the brain. The condition causes all the features displayed in the pictures of the Childe. Nowadays, the complaint can be successfully treated by a skilful surgical approach through the nose, which leaves no external scars. The patient needs only a few days in hospital and all the symptoms are arrested, normal proportions result and a happy and fertile lifespan ensues. In some cases, hormonal treatment in tablet form is all that is needed.

In future, acromegaly is likely to be diagnosed before it becomes embarrassingly obvious to the layman. So giants will remain an aspect of the past, even if not a figment of the imagination.

Mother Noblett and Old Ma Bushell (*c.* 1840–1900)

A Tale of Two Toffee Shops and a Famous Football Club

Do you like chewy sweets? Ever been to a football match? Admire clever business acumen? Here are two legendary women who knew a good(ison) way to make a profit. When Sheridan wrote *The Rivals*, he could not have known about the two retail competitors of Liverpool who would trade in the districts of Anfield and Everton. Well, retail competitors is a rather posh way to describe these grand old dames, but rivals they certainly were. If ever there was a 'Derby Match' it was that of Mother Noblett versus Old Ma Bushell and her gorgeous granddaughter.

Old Ma Bushell claimed that she invented the Everton Toffee. She had a natural flair for making creamy, chewy toffee in her little shop near St Domingo Church Sunday Football Club. Her talent was for warming just the right amount of sugar and butter together with a few other secret ingredients. Her sweets sold like hot cakes, especially before and after football matches.

As time went by, St Domingo changed its name to Everton Football Club, so that more players would be entitled to join the team. Even when the squad moved to Stanley Park in 1879 and subsequently to Priory Road, followed by a third move to Anfield, Old Ma Bushell's shop was still near enough to the match ground. She was ambitious. Her goal was to win enough custom to make a profit and then retire. The penalty of being situated in Anfield came in 1892, when the club's managers decided to move to a place called Mere Green Field, in Everton. They changed the name of the ground to Goodison Park but a change of name wasn't the problem for Ma. It was the distance. She found herself way off-side from the new venue. Her passing trade soon disappeared.

On the other hand, in Village Street, near the Queen's Hotel, there was a confectionery shop trading as Ye Anciente Everton Toffee House. Here, the owner was Mother Noblett, another dab-hand at tasty recipes. Her speciality was a minty concoction which somehow came out of the oven with white and black stripes. These sweets immediately scored a hit with the fans at the new venue, not only because of the deliciously refreshing taste but, by chance, the stripes echoed the design of the club's earlier strip.

Poor old Ma Bushell found herself well and truly wrong-footed. She scored an own goal as far as profits were concerned and she couldn't afford to transfer to new premises. Mother Noblett, however, found herself in the first division of sweet traders. Success and fortune came knocking on her door. But old Ma Bushell wasn't going to be relegated to the second division of has-beens. She dreamed up a scheme to tempt back her former fans.

Liverpool children offer an Everton Toffee to the Beatles' Eleanor Rigby. The sculpture is by Tommy Steele, who began his career in Liverpool and often returns.

With the help of her beautiful teenage granddaughter, she offered to provide free sweets to the crowd and a mascot for the club before every match. The directors accepted and young Jemima Bushell paraded her charms around the field, dressed in suitable colours and a very fetching hat. She carried grandma's shopping basket filled with the original toffees. These she lobbed over the barriers to the waiting spectators. After the final whistle, Granny and Jemima were ready at the exits with hundreds of little paper bags filled with the old favourites. These of course were not free. The men were already chewing and penniless before they reached Ma Bushell's shop!

The tradition continues to this day and a different 'Jemima' circles the field at every home match, throwing Everton Toffees to the eager crowd, while packets of toffees and mints are on sale in the souvenir shop.

Thanks to the internet and research into genuine historic documents, members of the present day Bushell family have traced their genealogy directly back to the original Ma Bushell. They have designed an impressive family tree, listing all their ancestors for over a hundred years and they are proud to carry on the surname of their intriguing ancestor.

Monsignor James Nugent
1822–1905

Father Nugent: 'Save the Child'

Immediately behind the elegant and imposing St George's Hall, Lime Street, Liverpool, there is a tiny park – St John's Gardens. Between its formal flower beds there are many bench seats, a military memorial and several impressive statues. Two of these, a matching pair, equal in size and similar in design, stand on either side of the gardens, both facing in the same direction and each featuring a child as well as the main figure. One depicts the philanthropist known to his admirers by the simple title of Father Nugent; the other bears the name of the revered benefactor, Canon Major Lester. As their titles suggest, one was Roman Catholic, his friend and fellow altruist a Protestant.

The history of the Irish Potato Famine has been told many times but the retribution for political mismanagement, coupled with natural disaster, was paid in full by Ireland's 'second capital', as Liverpool was known. Hundreds of thousands of destitute immigrants poured into the city at a time when it was already grossly overcrowded. Malnutrition and the lack of sanitation spread dysentery and cholera in epidemic proportions, with the result that thousands died and were thrown into unmarked paupers' graves. Yet, of almost equal gravity was the plague of religious bigotry in which Catholic and Orangemen fought bloody street-battles, adding to the death rate and the misery of already tragedy-stricken families and orphans in the poverty-stricken slums.

Two forward-thinking religious leaders rose above these destructive squabbles to set an example to their parishioners and to the town council. Each worked within the parameters of his own doctrine but each had a common objective, to preserve life and to improve the quality of that life. They met frequently, co-operated and co-ordinated their work and could often be seen walking around the diocese, arm in arm and deep in friendly conversation. The elder of these two by just seven years, James Nugent, was born at 22 Hunter Street, off Byrom Street. These two streets now form the border around the main building of the John Moores University.

James's father had been an Irish immigrant, who had started as an egg and fish dealer in St John's Market. By hard work and careful husbandry, he had built up the business and moved to a shop in Commutation Row, where the Transport and General Workers' Union building now stands. He then traded as the more affluent-sounding 'Fruiterer, Poulterer and Dealer in Game'. James was the first of nine children, and was twenty-six by the time his youngest sibling was born. Mary Nugent was an excellent mother. As well as attending lovingly to her own family, she set a saintly example, finding time to be 'ever the active and devoted helper of the poor and suffering. Many a bereaved family she has secretly helped in their distress; many a night she has spent with the sick and dying; many a loathsome case of disease has she dressed with her own hands. Unselfishness, gentleness and heroic energy stamped her character.'

As a youngster, James attended the Academy in Queen's Square, a Church of England establishment where James mixed with pupils of all denominations. On this site, the Marriott Hotel now stands, and next door is the pub named the Dr Duncan. Both of these buildings look out onto St John's Gardens where Father Nugent's statue stands.

James then went to Durham University and later completed his religious studies in Rome. He was a highly intelligent student, pleasant-looking with a clear, agreeable voice. He enjoyed amateur dramatics and quickly developed a talent for public speaking. Throughout his life, he retained his excellent vocal skills and remained articulate, eloquent, energetic, and charismatic. All of these qualities he used for the benefit of others and in the service of his faith.

When he returned to Liverpool, he found his parish drowning in the tragedy of disease and filthy living conditions. Ever the practical man, he immediately started a rescue operation, throwing a lifeline to the neglected and the destitute. He was instrumental in setting up night shelters and homes to cope with the thousands of barefoot orphans who had been forced to beg and steal in the streets. Disregarding his own safety, he followed his mother's example of realistic aid to the homeless and hopeless. At night, he would wander the unlit streets, gather up waifs and strays, guiding them to the refuge where his volunteers would feed and wash these poor little mites then give them bedding and warmth for the night. As time progressed, an understanding between Father Nugent and Canon Lester led to the practise of them meeting next morning and exchanging some of these tragic lost souls according to their creed (see p. 76).

With great spirit, stamina and dedication, Nugent created opportunities for the welfare and social development of these ill-fated infants, previously referred to as 'shadowy-eyed vermin', or 'street Arabs' by those with no understanding of their plight. Some orphans were taken into permanent care. For these, Father Nugent started a band, a choir, a music festival, a debating society, a reading club and a Boys' Guild. In 1850, he bought a house in Rodney Street to be used as a school, housing a gymnasium and library. He wrote for newspapers, became the editor and then the owner of the *Catholic Times*, providing work for the older boys, while at the same time using it to persuade the wealthy to contribute financial support for the homes. He also set up a scheme whereby struggling families received Christmas hampers if they could show a savings book with evidence of regular deposits, however small.

Father Nugent was an extraordinary pioneer battling against the bigotry of his times. By example, he built the bridges that Victorians needed to cross to reach more enlightened attitudes. For twenty years he worked as the first Catholic chaplain in a prison, Walton Gaol. He never condemned the inmates. He believed their crimes were forced upon them by their terrible circumstances. He was confessor, psychologist, friend and mentor to these unfortunates. He often spoke at public meetings where his eloquence helped to convince the wealthy and influential hierarchy that these criminals and 'incorrigible women' needed counselling not condemnation. Prisoners were treated with respect. Father Nugent understood that their only way of surviving was by the sharpness of their wits. His lectures were

almost theatrical performances, describing scenes he had witnessed in the streets or enacting conversations with prisoners. He wanted to bring alive to audiences his claims that training and guidance could transform even recidivists into honest citizens. In 1891, when a campaign against brothel-keepers made 800 prostitutes homeless, Nugent persuaded a nun who had served with Florence Nightingale, to open a refuge in Limekiln Lane, funded by benefactors of many beliefs. In 1897, he opened a home for unmarried mothers and their babies, in a mansion overlooking the Mersey, stressing that both partners were equally responsible for any offspring and that young girls were often victims not criminals.

At the age when many would consider retirement, Father Nugent travelled to America and Canada on protracted lecture tours, using the opportunity to take with him youngsters who might benefit from life in the New World. In the next few years, he arranged for many adolescents to join suitable families there and also in Australia.

His funeral in 1905 drew 10,000 mourners of all denominations and all walks of life. The city lowered its flags to half-mast and vowed never to forget this much loved and highly respected humanitarian. Today, the Nugent Care Society looks after the well-being of children and of disabled and disadvantaged people of all ages. Its work includes residential homes, special schools, adoption services and is a thriving and highly respected memorial to the pioneering work of Father Nugent.

Yoko Ono

Artist and Daughter-in-Law of Liverpool – the Ongoing Story

Everyone knows the story of The Beatles, their amazing talent, originality and engaging personalities. Their innovative approach to pop music took the world by storm and has lost none of its magical, mystical popularity with ensuing generations worldwide. Millions of biographical details have already been written about them. There are photographs and images everywhere. Several statues, sculptures and revered sites around Liverpool have become tourist magnets and Liverpool itself owes much of its fame to the Fab Four.

But what of today? Thanks in particular to Sir Paul McCartney and to Yoko Ono, the passing years have not consigned affectionate memories to the annals of history. Life on Merseyside in the twenty-first century is fuller, thanks to the enterprise and devotion of these two resilient survivors.

John Lennon's family home was in Allerton. Yoko Ono has embraced the whole city. John and Yoko met in 1966, at a preview of Yoko's work in a London art gallery. At first, Yoko did not recognise John as one of The Beatles but she was enchanted by his sense of humour and, in 1969, they were married in Gibraltar. Their son, Sean, was born in 1975 on John's birthday.

In 1980, Yoko had the terrifying and traumatic shock of seeing her beloved husband murdered before her very eyes. She later funded a memorial to John in Central Park, New York, near where he was killed. The memorial is known as Strawberry Fields. Since then, as well as her own work as a conceptual artist, Yoko has kept the eternal flame alight both in Liverpool and wherever she travels in the world. On what would have been John's sixty-sixth birthday, 9 October 2006, Yoko, whose name means Ocean Child, revealed her feelings about her acceptance of Liverpool City Council's invitation to become one of the Ambassadors for Liverpool 2008.

She said, 'I am so proud to support the Liverpool '08 Ambassador Programme! I fell in love with Liverpool the first time I came here in 1967 as an artist. When I arrived in Liverpool, the first thing that caught my eyes was the beautiful, old elegance of the city by the water. The professors at the art school were young and alert and all very hip to my stuff. When I performed at the Bluecoat Society, the place was filled with students who welcomed me warmly. A barely 5ft Asian artist who could have come from Mars for all they knew! It was an experience I would never forget.'

'After John's passing,' she continues, 'the people of Liverpool have been very kind to me. Now I feel like I am an adopted Liverpudlian. When I am in a far corner of the world having a hard time for one reason or another, I think of Liverpool and it calms my heart. It is the city that shaped the man I love: John Lennon, his poetry, his sense of humour, his northern resilience to hard life.'

'I am also from an old city by the water called Tokyo, which also gave me a sense of poetry, humour and Asian resilience to life's hard blows. We met and we fell in love. I know that part of John's heart was always with Liverpool, his hometown. He was a proud Liverpudlian. When I prayed that Liverpool would be chosen for 2008 I knew that John was with me all the way.'

Yoko keeps John's spirit alive in many different ways, all to the benefit of the people of his own city. The change of name from Speke Airport to John Lennon Airport has drawn worldwide attention to its thriving expansion, lifted its international status and brought social and economic benefit to the area. The Yellow Submarine sculpture welcomes and delights young travellers, setting an air of expectancy from the outset.

As well as securing 'Mendips' into the care of the National Trust, Yoko has guaranteed that the home where John grew up and where the Beatles were born will now remain historically correct in every detail. This boosts the number of local tourist attractions available to visitors from far and wide.

John's childhood school, at Dovedale Road, which intersects with Penny Lane, has recently been the grateful recipient of computers, educational and play equipment, general refurbishments and a complete make-over for its outdoor area, all thanks to personal gifts from Yoko.

In 2000, Yoko dedicated a John Lennon Museum in the town of Saitma in Japan, and in 2001, Liverpool University awarded her an Honorary Doctorate of Law.

Yoko with a young patient at the John Lennon Imagine Centre in Alder Hey Children's Hospital.

Her own artistic contribution to Liverpool's cultural expansion received a mixed reception in 2004. Her huge posters of female anatomy provoked much controversy but at least people took notice and discussed her iconoclastic style. Artists from previous centuries have often been misunderstood by their contemporaries, only to be appreciated later.

In 2007, as part of her world travels, Yoko brought awareness of Liverpool to Reykjavik, Iceland, where she dedicated a new memorial called the Imagine Peace Tower, on the Isle of Videry. She also mounted a Lennon-themed art exhibition, which has toured galleries worldwide.

Perhaps the gesture most likely to touch hearts in the North-West is Yoko's decision to become an active patron of Alder Hey's Imagine Appeal in West Derby. By her personal visits and financial support she has raised the profile of one of Europe's leading medical centres. Madeleine Fletcher, Imagine's Senior Fundraising Manager says, 'We are so grateful to Yoko for all her wonderful help. Her involvement means so much to us in every way. I'm sure we shall go on from strength to strength with her as our figurehead and our little patients will benefit in so many ways.'

In her acceptance of the Liverpool '08 Ambassadorship, Yoko wrote, 'Liverpool, Liverpool. Stay magical and beautiful. Your future is whatever you wish to make it. I love you . . . Yoko.'

Sir Simon Rattle

Child Prodigy and World-Famous Conductor

Liverpool College, close to Sefton Park, Mossley Hill, was the alma mater of several of Liverpool's most outstanding citizens, among them, Noel and Christopher Chavasse, Sir Rex Harrison and, at a much later date, Sir Simon Rattle. Simon spent his formative years in Mossley Hill. He and his sister grew up in a stimulating and cultural home, frequently surrounded by fascinating people

from all parts of the world. Their parents, Pauline and Denis Rattle were gregarious and generously hospitable. As well as being a businessman and a teacher, Denis was the chairman of the northern branch of the English Speaking Union, which fosters global harmony as well as close association and friendship among all English language countries. Overseas guests to Liverpool were always welcome at the Rattle home, for both informal parties and for longer visits. The family also took a particular interest in Liverpool's highly acclaimed School of Tropical Medicine. They raised funds through social occasions, lecture courses and by encouraging talented young Merseysiders to use their creative abilities to write and perform musical revues in aid of the School of Tropical Medicine and for Mersey Kidney Research.

As a young teenager, Simon was always an enthusiastic member of the audience at these shows. His father was eventually awarded the OBE for his services to international concord. Simon's own talent had already shown itself at a very early age. When his father played twentieth-century American music and jazz on the piano, Simon, hardly more than a toddler, could tap out the rhythm in perfect timing. At the age of ten, Simon joined the Merseyside Youth Orchestra and appeared as a percussionist with the Royal Liverpool Philharmonic Orchestra. While still a young teenager, he joined the National Youth Orchestra and began to specialise in conducting. He also created a new classical group, the Liverpool Sinfonia. His next move was to the Royal Academy of Music, winning the John Player International Conductors' Competition at the age of nineteen.

In 1974, the Bournemouth Symphony Orchestra welcomed him as assistant conductor. He stayed with them until returning to Liverpool in 1977 as assistant conductor. From 1980–1, Simon decided to enrol at St Ann's College, Oxford, where he added the study of English Literature and Language to his musical and academic qualifications.

Several major American orchestras wooed him and the Los Angeles Philharmonic Orchestra persuaded him to take up the post of principal guest conductor, with frequent visits until 1994.

While Simon was still only twenty-four, he joined the City of Birmingham Symphony Orchestra as principal conductor and musical adviser. The consequence was electrifying. Over the coming years, Simon Rattle transformed an average regional orchestra into a worldwide phenomenon, producing a metamorphosis beyond all expectation. With charisma, boundless energy, amazing depth of knowledge and astonishing empathy with the works of classical composers, he built up an international reputation second to none. He and his musicians were invited to tour North America, the Far East and much of Europe.

At the same time, Rattle was becoming well-known on television, giving a series of musically illustrated talks. Interviews and articles in the media were eagerly sought after and his photograph could double ticket sales for any event. Hardly a week passed without yet another shot of his ready smile and signature mop of Beethoven-like curly hair. Baton raised, he is easily the most recognisable conductor in the classical world. In 1993, he was awarded the Mont Blanc de la Culture for devotion to cultural endeavour and, in 1994, he was honoured with a knighthood for his services to music. In 1995, the French Minister of Culture honoured him as an Officier des Arts et des Lettres. He also received the Toepfer Foundation of Hamburg's Shakespeare Prize for outstanding contribution to arts within the framework of Europe's Cultural Heritage. In 1997, he was the *BBC Music* magazine's choice for outstanding achievement and was also decorated with the RSA Albert Medal for outstanding contribution to tourism and involvement in educational and community services.

A most prestigious appointment, in 2002, to become chief conductor and artistic director with the Berlin Philharmonic Orchestra has increased Sir Simon's international fame and given him much creative satisfaction. He and his present instrumentalists are the aristocracy of the classical world, prompting guest soloists to vie for the privilege of appearing with the orchestra.

Sir Simon has been married twice. He has two sons from his first marriage, no children from his second and a third son from his present partnership.

Within hours, tickets were sold out for Sir Simon's much longed-for guest appearance in his home city, at a celebratory concert during Liverpool's Capital of Culture Year, 2008. Many hundreds of local classical music lovers were left disappointed and can only hope that a return visit might be arranged for a later date.

Red Rum

'He Jumped into the Hearts of Millions'

In the world of horse racing, there are dedicated aficionados who follow every meeting in the calendar and can quote every detail about the trainers, the owners, the conditions, the pedigrees and the odds. They even go riding at every opportunity themselves. Then there are the betting shop punters who never go near a race course but who make a 'killing' once in a while and a loss most days of the week. There are syndicates and work colleagues who join in sweepstakes just for the fun of it. There are dedicated followers of fashion who don't go to see the race but go to be seen at the race course. And there are little old ladies who only have a flutter once a year – always on the Grand National. They know absolutely nothing about horses or tic-tac men or the Tote or the evens and odds. But the Grand National is like Christmas to them. It only comes once a year but it is so special, it's a chance to splash out and have a bit of fun.

All of these people have, however, one thing in common. You can bet that they all have the fondest memories of one phenomenal animal, Red Rum. No other horse has ever evoked such loyalty and such a wealth of affection in every section of the public. It has been said that he was the first horse ever to have star quality and to become a nationwide celebrity in his own right.

This handsome gelding was born in Ireland, lived most of his life on Merseyside, loved the beach at Southport and was ridden at Aintree many times.

Red Rum. How did he get his name? Well, his father was called Quorum and his mother's name was Mared. Theirs was an arranged marriage simply because their owners were friendly with each other. Now, if you take the last three letters from each of the parent's names (ladies first, of course) they spell Red Rum. Easy.

There was no great plan behind the mating. No particular wonders were expected of the offspring. In fact, Mared was so temperamental that she would work up a froth even before entering the parade ground and she only ever won one race. When it was time for her colt to be sold, his stiff, almost limping gait didn't look at all promising and he fetched only a very moderate fee.

The first time his trainer, Ginger McCain, saw him, he was actually looking for jumpers and thought that Red Rum could never be anything more than a runner, so he walked away uninterested. On a subsequent occasion though, McCain did buy him, on behalf of owner Noel Le Mare. The stable lad at McCain's stables in Upper Aughton Road was a boy from Birkdale called Lee Mack, who grew up to be a famous television comedian.

McCain made use of the wide open spaces of the firm, flat sand on Southport Beach to take Rummy for his exercise and training. It was here that Rummy decided he liked to gallop through the shallows of the sea. The salt water seemed to bring about a marked improvement in the condition of the champion's foot. So this treat became a regular preparation for all subsequent Grand Nationals.

Red Rum's widespread popularity arises from his charismatic personality, his natural good looks and his superlative achievements. In spite of suffering from a crippling foot disease known as pedalostitis, for which there is no known cure, this magnificent member of the equine family boasts a track record as follows:

1967	Won at Aintree on the flat.
1973	Won the Grand National.
1974	Won the Grand National and the Scottish Grand National.
1975	Came second in the Grand National.
1976	Came second in the Grand National.
1977	Won the Grand National.

But Red Rum wouldn't boast! Two of the most endearing qualities were his sweet nature and his lack of erratic behaviour. In total, he had five trainers and twenty different jockeys and none of them had a bad word to say about him. He was the Dixie Dean of the racing world.

His third triumph in the Grand National was a stupendous win by twenty-five lengths, at the age of twelve. He also won prestigious races at other courses. Altogether, he won three flat races, three hurdles and twenty-one steeplechases. His hat-trick of three Grand National victories plus two second places created a record unbeaten to this day.

After a hairline fracture brought about his retirement, he wasn't put out to grass. He led the opening parade at Aintree for many years, he was engaged to open supermarkets, he switched on the illuminations at Blackpool and he saw the jumps at Becher's Brook and the Chair reduced in height after protests at the many injuries and deaths resulting from this most punishing of races. When he died in 1995, even the bookies who had lost so much money owing to this phenomenal pulling power, were truly sad at his passing.

He is buried at the winning post at Aintree, where there is also a life-size statue of him. Another, smaller statue stands in the Wayfarers Arcade on Lord Street, Southport. A new equine statue, in Liverpool City Centre, of a high-spirited horse, must also have been inspired by Red Rum. He is still the most famous animal on Merseyside.

Anne Robinson

The Traveller who says 'I'm Proud to be a Liverpudlian'

Have you ever wondered how Anne Robinson could so easily morph from being the people's friend and champion, wearing a nice little cardigan on *Watchdog*, into the severe Queen of Mean of *The Weakest Link*? How did the warm and chatty presenter of *Points of View* become the black-clad virago with a sarcastic insult for every one of her victims?

Look no further than the example set by her mother, who ruled the household like a cross between an elegant female version of Alan Sugar and a self-funding Imelda Marcos, equally go-getting and in no mood to suffer fools gladly.

Long ago, this woman's ancestors had arrived in Liverpool from Ireland. It was around 1846, after the potato famine, when Father Nugent, Kitty Wilkinson and Dr Duncan were each valiantly striving to alleviate the dire poverty and appalling conditions that led to such widespread fever and death in Liverpool. The indomitable genes must have already been present in this Gaelic family, because they struggled and survived when so many others succumbed.

Many decades later, their descendant, Anne Robinson's mother, Anne Wilson, determined to put her humble background behind her and emulate the wealthy upper classes who were living on the outskirts of Liverpool, in Blundellsands and Crosby. She married a kind-hearted, popular schoolteacher who later became a captain in the Royal Artillery. During and after the Second World War, Mrs Robinson set herself up in a butcher's stall at St John's Market in the city centre. With single-minded determination and unfailing hard work, she gradually became by far the most prosperous trader in the covered market. Her odd little maxim was 'Up at six and out by five!' Her business acumen was instinctive and enterprising to say the least. Profits soared.

By the time young Anne and her brother, Peter, arrived on the scene, the Robinsons were a two-car family (usually Bentleys, Rovers or Daimlers). This was at a time, in the post-war austerity years, when most families, even middle-class ones, had no car at all. Mrs Robinson could afford to dress in the height of fashion, bought at George Henry Lee's, in the heart of town. Her pearls and diamonds came from Boodle and Dunthorne's, still the most exclusive jewellers in Liverpool. She also developed a taste for plenty of expensive wines and other alcoholic drinks. This family holidayed in the South of France, while others were lucky to make it as far as North Wales.

The sale of oven-ready rabbits, chickens and turkeys was the basis of the family fortune. In the school holidays, young Anne helped her mother on the stall, even to the extent of gutting the poultry. Term-time, meanwhile, was spent as a boarder at Farnborough Hill Convent in Hampshire, and later, at a high-class finishing school, Les Ambassadrices in Paris and after that at the Gregg Secretarial College in Liverpool.

At the convent school, Anne learned everyday essentials such as how to curtsey and how to read aloud while standing on a chair! In Paris, the 'uniform' consisted of expensive evening dresses, ski-wear, different outfits for every activity whether it was in the art studio, the cordon bleu kitchen or at the many fashion shows. Anne was less than thrilled at mixing with debutantes and social climbers but her mother was delighted. At the Gregg College, Anne learned typing, which proved genuinely useful when she later became a journalist. Reading aloud under difficult circumstances also came in handy as practice for using an autocue in television studios. The perfect curtsey proved most effective on being introduced to Prince Edward. He protested that it was totally unnecessary but Anne told him that her mother had paid many thousands of pounds for this and it was nice to make use of it at last!

Anne's early career was in journalism. A lucky quirk of fate put her in the right place at the right time to file an exclusive scoop on Brian Epstein's unexpected death. This coup led to a job on the *Daily Mail* and became the stepping-stone to further fortunes.

Anne's first husband, the father of their stunningly beautiful daughter, Emma, was Charlie Wilson. So Anne Robinson became Anne Wilson, echoing her mother's maiden name. In another respect, too, she was like her mother. Anne soon found herself drawn into the boozy lifestyle of the press. Following in her mother's unsteady footsteps, she fell into the self-destructive routines of an alcoholic. It affected her work, her marriage and her life in general. The younger Mrs Wilson was destined to return to her unmarried state when it became apparent that her marriage was ill-matched and not what either partner had expected. Much to Anne's chagrin, she lost her daughter, Emma, to the custody of her ex-husband. As she explains in her autobiography, the Victorian expression 'Mother's ruin' was true for Anne. It ruined her life as a mother to Emma.

A change of job took Anne Robinson to the *Sunday Times*. She recalls this as the favourite period of her career. Health problems, however, were eventually the cause of her leaving journalism for while. Alcohol, so long a friend, turned out to be a bitter enemy.

When Anne eventually met the man who was to become her second husband, John Penrose, they moved to Rome where he was a foreign correspondent. But soon Anne was to return to Liverpool, trying to sort out her life and personal problems. It was a difficult time and she often felt that she was taking one step forward and whole mile of tottering steps back, but again a lucky chance came her way. She found a job with the *Liverpool Daily Post and Echo*. With a struggle, her talent and determination proved stronger than her inherent addiction. Within a short time, she was given a regular column of her own. Over the years, Anne has worked on most of the newspapers that come readily to mind, including the post of assistant editor at the *Daily Mirror*. Her articles were always fearlessly outspoken in their condemnation of injustice. Gradually, she moved into television while still producing her own weekly column at the *Daily Mirror*, prophetically nicknamed 'The Wednesday Witch'.

Then along came *Watchdog* for the BBC, gaining an enormous audience. *The Weakest Link* brought her untold fame and fortune. It was copied worldwide, with clone-like presenters slavishly copying Anne's forbidding garb, red hair, severe glasses and scathing remarks. Worldwide, that is, except in the United States. The wise Americans decided that Anne herself was the only person who could carry off the delicate balance between sadistic inquisitor and fashion icon.

Her mother would be overjoyed at the riches Anne could now command. Sadly, Mrs Robinson's last years were blighted by the tragedy of Alzheimer's Disease. Anne is now one of the Vice-Presidents of the Alzheimer's Association.

The interest in education that Anne inherited from her father emerges when Anne co-hosts the general knowledge questionnaire *Test The Nation*. He would be so proud to see her as more of a schoolteacher than a domineering interrogator. Both parents would probably find it hard to understand why a chance remark about Liverpool's neighbours in Wales, supposedly said as a joke, should cause Anne to be accused of racism. But they would be amused to see her taking the mickey out of herself in a *Doctor Who* episode as a robotic creature called Ann Droid. They would also be more than delighted that she was invited by St Andrews University to stand for the post of Rector. Her investiture as an Honorary Fellow of John Moores University, Liverpool, was better than winning any quiz show jackpot. It bestowed upon Anne the honour denied in earlier years by her mother's tunnel vision, withholding from Anne the university education given to her brother. But it does combine her mother's desire for status symbols with her father's genuine love of scholarship.

'It's all in the genes, you know,' as Anne would say, with a wink.

William Roscoe 1753–1831

Advocate of Freedom – Abolitionist of Slavery

Liverpool European Capital of Culture – 2008. Many present-day citizens of Merseyside, including several mentioned in this book, have worked tirelessly and contributed greatly towards the achievement of this honour. One other person deserves special acknowledgement although he was born 255 years before this festival event. However, he was a visionary, foreseeing some of Liverpool's destiny, an enthusiast, contributing to Liverpool's cultural heritage and a campaigner, striving to influence Liverpool's ethical conscience. He is known as both the 'founder of Liverpool's culture' and as 'Liverpool's greatest citizen'.

William Roscoe was the only son of Elizabeth and William Roscoe Snr, who owned and lived in a tavern called the Old Bowling Green, with an adjacent market garden. The inn and its grounds were situated at the top of Mount Pleasant, Liverpool, almost on the site of the present-day Everyman Theatre, the Medical Institution and the Catholic Cathedral. On the smallholding, Mr Roscoe grew potatoes and other vegetables for sale to the public. During young William's childhood, this area was at the very edge of the city, bordering on countryside, with wide open views of the River Mersey and the Wirral. Inland, there were woods and farmlands as far as the villages of West Derby, Woolton and Hale.

From his father, the boy learned the love of nature and all things rural. From his mother he inherited an appreciation of literature, poetry, art, foreign languages and the dignity of all mankind – worldwide. When he was six years old, he used to walk down the hill towards the waterfront to a school in Paradise Street. His education lasted only six years, as he left school at the age of twelve to help in his father's market garden. From then on, he was determined to learn as much as he could by educating himself. Deprived of the books at school, he immediately bought one of his own. As the years went by, he managed to build up, book by book, an enormous and most prestigious library of interesting and valuable volumes. Encouraged by his mother, he began writing poetry in the elegant and imaginative style fashionable at the time. When he was fifteen he found himself a job in a book store and from there he became a clerk-apprentice to a solicitor in Church Street.

At home he continued to study widely in many subjects. He began to illustrate his own poems and he discovered a love of classical paintings and European history. He

also became acquainted with a circle of friends with strong social consciences. From an untutored youth, he turned himself into one of the most knowledgeable, talented and scholarly figures of his era. In particular, he developed a high regard for Italian art, language and literature. As he hardly ever journeyed outside Liverpool and never once travelled abroad, he relied on the help of a friend to bring back Florentine paintings and other artefacts for the fine collection he eventually built up.

Roscoe had a particularly happy marriage, dedicating love poems to his wife, Jane Julia, well into middle-age, mentioning the thousands of kisses they still enjoyed. As they had ten children, they moved several times to larger premises in Dingle,

Islington, to the stately home Allerton Hall, and finally to a smaller residence in Toxteth's Lodge Lane. As well as becoming a self-taught historian and writing books which were translated into many languages, he also became a lawyer, a banker and an MP for Liverpool. Roscoe was a staunch Unitarian, a denomination which, at that time, debarred him from certain important posts within the borough. Rigid tenets were the order of the day and, although he was a reformer, he would not flout existing laws, however preposterous, for his own advantage.

Roscoe's life spanned a period in Liverpool's history which he and other enlightened figures considered utterly shameful. Liverpool merchants were building up fortunes for themselves via the iniquitous slave trade. Many were not actively cruel themselves, but they could see no wrong in the inhuman degradation of their fellow men as a method of lining their own pockets. They were possibly able to delude themselves that this atrocious trade was legitimate, simply because they never saw the evidence of their utter callousness with their own eyes. The slaves did not come into Liverpool at all. There was a maritime triangle of commerce. Liverpool exported manufactured goods to Guinea. When unloaded, the ships then took on board slaves and set sail direct for the West Indies, where the men were sold to the highest and most unscrupulous bidders. The return voyage brought spices, sugar and rum into Liverpool. Ignorance was, of course, no excuse, and Roscoe, along with other like-minded humanitarians, fought consistently to bring about the abolition of this evil exploitation. To reach a wider audience than just the committees in his home town, Roscoe used his talents as a poet. In 1777, he published a long, descriptive poem in which he attacked the slave trade, knowing that it would reach a wide readership far beyond Merseyside.

He wrote:

> Shame to Mankind! But shame to Britons most,
> Who all the sweets of Liberty can boast;
> Yet, deaf to every human claim, deny
> That bliss to others, which they themselves enjoy.
>
> Yet whence these horrors? This inhuman rage,
> That brands with blackest infamy the age?
> Is it (our varied interests disagree),
> That Britain sinks if Afric's sons be free?
> No. Hence a few superfluous stores we claim,
> That tempt our greed, but increase our shame.
>
> Blest were the days ere Foreign Climes were known,
> Our wants were less and our wealth our own;
> Our drink, the beverage of the crystal flood,
> Not madly purchased by another's blood.
> Ere the wide-spreading ills of Trade began,
> Or luxury trampled on the rights of man.

He followed this with another called 'The Wrongs of Africa', in which he wrote:

> Form'd with the same capacity of pain,
> The same desire of pleasure and of ease,
> Why feels not man for man? When nature shrinks
> From the slight puncture of an insect's sting,
> Faints if not screen'd from sultry suns, and pines
> Beneath the hardship of one hour's delay
> Of needful nutriment;
> How shall this sufferer man, his fellow doom
> To ills he mourns, or spurns at? Tear with stripes
> His quivering flesh; with hunger and with thirst
> Waste his emaciate frame? In ceaseless toils
> Exhaust his vital powers; and bind his limbs
> In galling chains?

Roscoe became the leader of the abolition movement in Liverpool, but made himself very unpopular with the heartless rich merchants of the town. During his term of office as MP for Liverpool, there were rioting protests at his policies and he was physically attacked by ordinary seamen whose livelihood depended upon the slave ships.

Roscoe also supported the original ideals of the French Revolution but was later appalled at the fanaticism and hysterical cruelty it engendered. In 1807 he was rewarded with the knowledge that the slave trade had at last been outlawed, due in no small part to his campaigning and his vote in Parliament. Legal procedure had triumphed over the shameful crimes perpetrated by his contemporaries. Existing slaves, however, did not gain their freedom until 1833.

For Liverpool itself, he used his great loves of both literature and nature. He helped to found both the Athenaeum Library, contributing many books himself, and the Botanical Gardens as well as presenting a generous section of his art collection to the Walker Art Gallery. A monument to him now stands in Renshaw Street but his greatest memorial is the multicultural city he fostered and the people of today who consistently throng its highly esteemed theatres, art galleries, libraries, concert halls and intellectual societies. A city where all ethnic groups and creeds live and work together in every neighbourhood and occupation; and whose society, after some deeply dark times, is enjoying a resurgence of culture, conscience and hope for the future.

For several years, the Roscoe Lectures, organised by the Federation for Citizenship in conjunction with the John Moores University and under the leadership of Lord Alton, with financial help from Rex Makin, has arranged a series of lectures at which worldwide figures from all political, religious and cultural persuasions are invited to speak on their interpretation of citizenship. The meetings, held mainly in St George's Hall, are always full to capacity, drawing audiences from every age group and all walks of life. Each meeting also celebrates the special contribution to the community made by different schoolboys and girls in a variety of ways. A presentation to the young citizens precedes each lecture.

Bill Shankly 1913–81

Football Legend and Creator of the Modern Liverpool Football Club

From Alder Hey Children's Hospital in West Derby, walk or drive the full length of Eaton Road and you will come to the Bill Shankly Playing Fields, divided into several pitches and used every weekend by scores of appreciative youngsters. They might be too young to remember the man himself, but you can be sure they know everything about this renowned football manager and much-loved icon. Life at the Anfield stadium and the Melwood practice ground only really started when this dyed-in-the-wool Scottish Scouser arrived on the scene in 1959.

One of the best-loved Scousers of all time, the one with the deeply ingrained Scottish accent, Bill Shankly, was born in Glenbuck, Ayrshire, a mining village. He was one of ten children. Mr Shankly Snr, like every other man in the vicinity, was a miner. Apart from the grocer's shop, the bakery or the pawn-broker's, there was no alternative to going down the pit. Football was simply a leisure activity, restricted to Saturday afternoons.

But Bill had his sights on the world of professional football. He lived and breathed the game and began to build up an unparalleled inventory of teams, players and tactics. His own skill as a player enabled him to escape the coal-face to play wing-half for Carlisle, then Preston and Scotland. He was deprived of stardom on the pitch when his career was interrupted by the Second World War. Undeterred, post-war Bill became a manager, first at Carlisle, then at Grimsby, Workington and Huddersfield.

From the moment he set foot on the Anfield turf, he knew he had come home. 'I was born for Liverpool and Liverpool was born for me' was his firm belief. With his optimistic personality he soon developed into a superb motivator and inspirational father figure. Before his arrival, the Reds were lucky to be called mediocre. They were floundering in the quagmire of the Second Division. The only Merseyside team of any note was Everton, with their fantastic reputation built up in the days of superstar Dixie Dean.

Apart from the poor results, the stadium and practice ground were both in a sad state of repair. Morale was low and ticket sales were suffering. But Liverpool and Shankly were a marriage made in heaven. No sooner had the first whistle blown than Bill set about a complete transformation of the philosophy of the club. Starting at the roots, he retrained the support staff, pruned out the weaker players, grafted in three of his compatriots with good reputations, striker Ian St John, centre-back Ron Yeats and goalie Tommy Lawrence. He fed the sapling team with compliments, humour and galvanising determination. The fans watched with hope in their hearts, as it grew and blossomed.

Bill's rapport with Liverpool fans was immediate. He felt that he was on their wavelength and they instinctively responded. In return, Bill made it known how much he appreciated their support. 'The fans here are the greatest,' he said. 'They know the game and they know what they want to see. The people on the Kop make you feel great – yet humble. There's only one way to go,' he told the team in a training session, 'up!'

Very soon, owing to his obsessional devotion, his rebuilt team secured promotion in the 1961/2 season and within two years they were the League Champions. During the next decade the Reds stormed through to more and more triumphs, the FA Cup, a second League Championship and several European conquests, crowned by carrying off the UEFA Cup in the same 1973 season as the Championship.

Bill's witty approach to the game was sometimes premeditated, as when he turned up with a bulky carrier bag and asked one of his officials at a derby match to hand out extra toilet rolls to the Blues when they arrived. 'Here, give them one each,' he instructed. 'They'll need it when they see what a brilliant team we're fielding today.'

'The Anfield plaque,' he declared on another occasion, 'is there to remind our lads who they're playing for and to terrify the opposition and remind them who they're playing against.' Occasionally, his humour was unintentional. 'The problem with you, son,' he complained to a Melwood trainee, 'all your brains are in your head.'

He wouldn't allow any skiving. 'You haven't got a broken leg,' he told an injured player, 'it's all in your head.' Bill was great believer in equality. The workload was shared among everyone. Stars were encouraged to pass the ball to team mates if it was in the interest of the game, rather then hogging the limelight and possibly letting a split-second opportunity slip away. If a decision went against the Reds, Shankly would growl, 'The trouble with refs, they know the rules but they don't understand the game.' When secretly viewing a recommended new signing, Bill was told how valuable the player was but he wasn't impressed. 'A hundred thousand wouldn't buy him,' he was assured. 'Yeah, and I'm one of the hundred thousand who wouldn't buy him,' came the instant reply.

Considered by many to be the greatest manager of all time, Bill was honoured with the OBE. When Adidas decided to present him with a golden boot in recognition of the fame he had brought to Liverpool FC, Bob Paisley took the phone call. 'They want to know your shoe size,' he called out to his boss. 'A gold boot, you say? Well, if it's gold, I take size twenty-eight,' was the quick response.

Shankly had laid the foundation of such an indomitable side that when he combined the 3–0 destruction of Newcastle in 1974 FA Cup with the announcement of his own retirement, the team and fans were inconsolable. But Shankly made a gift to his successor, Bob Paisley, of a side that could and did fight on to even greater fame and fortune in the coming seasons.

The Shankly Gates at Anfield and the bronze statue of the man himself in triumphant pose, ensure that his great spirit, as in life, walks on with hope in his heart and will 'Never Walk Alone'.

Alison Steadman
Seriously Humorous Actress

If you happened to be in the area of Walton, Liverpool, some years ago and happened to notice a beautiful young blonde girl going into the Probation Office on a regular basis, you might be forgiven for wondering what offence she had committed. She seemed to be there nearly every day. Was she on parole, reporting to her personal probation officer? What a pity! So young and so attractive, too!

A couple of years later, when she was no longer such a daily visitor, you might have wondered what had become of her. Was she back inside, or maybe just going straight? Then you'd think, 'Well, forget it. Probably never see her again.'

What a surprise, then, when Miss Steadman, who had actually been working at Walton Probation Office and had gone straight – to Drama School in London and then gone 'straight' in the theatrical meaning of being cast in classical dramas – eventually turned up on your television screen and has been there ever since, with several recent appearances including *Miss Marple*, *The Dinner Party*, *Gavin and Stacey*, *Fanny Hill* and *The Omid Djalili Show*.

Alison, born in Anfield, attended Pinehurst Road Primary School. Later, when her family moved to the south end of the city, she became a pupil at Childwall Valley High School for Girls.

With her good looks and natural flair for wicked impersonations, it soon became clear where her talents would take her. How fortunate that, as well as Liverpool having a good probation service, it also had the splendid Everyman Theatre in Hope Street and the Liverpool Youth Theatre.

Alison recalls, 'Liverpool Youth Theatre was my life for four years. In particular I would like to thank and pay tribute to my teachers Tony Joy, Jim Wiggins and Mildred Spencer. Between them, they ran the Youth Group between 1960 and 1970. They gave me the confidence to apply for drama school in London. Without their help and encouragement, I couldn't have done what I've done. They helped me on my way. I also loved my Everyman days. The opportunities there were wonderful, with Alan Dosser directing and John McGrath writing. At the Liverpool Playhouse, I was lucky enough to work with actor-director Tony Colgate, to whom I also owe a great debt of thanks.'

Alison also has fond memories of her two years at the probation office. As well as the fun she had going to the Cavern during her lunch hours and following Paul McCartney for his autograph, her colleagues were so understanding, encouraging and generous. 'When I left they all clubbed together and bought the books I would need at drama school, to help me.'

Help also came from Liverpool City Council. Alison needed a grant to study at the 'East 15' Drama College in London. The education committee awarded her this without hesitation. Alison says, with emphasis, 'Thank you Liverpool!'

There are two other very important people who mean the world to Alison. She says, 'I want to thank my mother and father, Marjorie and George Steadman, for their love and support. They always believed in me.'

That belief has been well and truly justified. Alison quickly won such sought-after roles as Ophelia in *Hamlet* and Sandy in *The Prime Of Miss Jean Brody*. Other stimulating and quirky parts soon followed. Notably the unforgettable Candice-Marie, trailing through the fields in the craziest camping holiday ever, in Mike Leigh's wonderfully titled *Nuts In May*. Candice-Marie and her boyfriend certainly were 'nuts'.

This early success set the benchmark for many subsequent castings. In a list of credits far longer than your arm, it is obvious that writers and directors such as Alan Ayckbourn, Dawn French, Lewis Gilbert and fellow Liverpudlian, the highly acclaimed Jude Kelly, appreciate Alison's bubbly sense of humour and knack of bringing out the absurd in a character.

Critics agree. Alison won the Olivier Award for her part as the over-the-top mother in *The Rise and Fall of Little Voice*, two BAFTA nominations, one for *The Singing Detective* and one for *Fat Friends*. She also won the *Evening Standard* Award for best actress for her portrayal of the preposterous Beverley in Mike Leigh's *Abigail's Party*. Thanks to their teamwork, this West End success won plaudits all round. Their excellent rapport was strengthened by the fact that at the time, they were married to each other.

Like Marilyn Monroe, Alison has made a career of combining 'incredibly sexy with funny'. Her Liverpool background came to the fore as Shirley Valentine's best friend in Willy Russell's film of that name, as well as in the short-lived television series called *The Wackers*. *Fat Friends* stretched Alison's image to suit the part and Jane Austen must surely have created the exorbitant Mrs Bennett in *Pride and Prejudice* especially with Alison in mind. Hers was the definitive portrayal.

Can your arm stretch any longer? I hope so, because as well as 'crazy' (she is also voice-over artist for children's cartoons and *Grumpy Old Women*) and sexy, Alison also does 'academic' and 'public spirit'. Liverpool University honoured her with a Doctorate of Literature. She has an Honorary MA from the University of East London, another Honorary Doctorate of Literature from the University of Essex and an OBE for her Services to Drama. She has also joined with Helen Mirren, Patrick Stewart and fellow Liverpudlians Phil Redmond and Jimmy McGovern, to support a scheme hoping to re-create Shakespeare's Cockpit Theatre in Prescot, Merseyside. If successful, it will also house a cinema, dance studio, exhibition area and restaurant and will bring hundreds of new jobs to the district. Prescot and Liverpool would be delighted to welcome Alison to open such a prestigious addition to Merseyside's cultural scene.

George Stubbs 1724–1806
Self-Taught Genius of the Art World

From 1745 to 1751, young medical students and nurses in York County Hospital received their instruction in anatomy, midwifery and post-natal care from 'an expert and experienced doctor'? One would think so. But no. Their tutor was a youthful artist and an unqualified one at that. He was nevertheless regarded as a greater authority on anatomy than the surgeons around him and was soon to provide the detailed illustrations for an educational textbook on midwifery.

Eventually to gain the fine reputation as the greatest British animal painter, George Stubbs was born in Liverpool, the son of a leather merchant. His talent and interest in art showed itself at an very early age. Even as a child he was fascinated by anatomy, taking particular interest in the human and animal skeleton. As a boy he persuaded a local doctor to give him some bones to draw and in York, the town surgeon actually provided him with a corpse of a woman who had died at the age of 110. Far from being repelled, George was intrigued. Using his scientific and artistic talents he first painted a portrait of the woman and then dissected the cadaver in a systematic manner.

Never did he receive any education in medicine or surgery and his only formal training in art was a brief apprenticeship to a painter and engraver, whose idea of tuition was to force the young prodigy to make copies of the works of established artists. George soon left and set himself up as a portrait painter, while still exploring anatomy. He travelled towards the north of England, first to Wigan, then Leeds and Hull, financed by his natural ability as an artist. He then settled in York where his competence was enough to gain him his post as medical lecturer.

His artistic reputation began to spread and commissions for portraits came his way. By 1755 he was able to afford a visit to Italy in order to acquaint himself with Greco-Roman architecture, but he was still convinced that the works of nature were more beautiful than the works of man. Returning via the northern tip of Morocco and staying for a while at Ceuta, opposite Gibraltar, he chanced to see a lion pounce on a white Barbary horse. The moonlit scene had an emotional effect upon him and he produced a series of paintings on the theme of this dramatic attack. The subject immediately caught the imagination of the public and increased his popularity.

In addition to his creative talent, Stubbs had a flair for business. He realised that his skill at equine depiction could be useful to members of the Jockey Club, as detailed works of reference on breeding and pedigree. His idea was sound and in 1756, having found himself a steady girlfriend, Mary Spencer, with whom he had a son, George Townley Stubbs, he rented a farmhouse in a Lincolnshire village.

117

Mary lived with him and was happy to assist in his research. In one of the barns, they constructed an apparatus to support the body of a dead horse, in a standing position. Stubbs then dissected it meticulously, sketching the muscular and skeletal functions in great detail. As there was no one locally to engrave plates from his drawings, he drew on his former training from his youth, made his own engravings and was then able to publish and sell a portfolio of authentic and accurate illustrations, entitled *The Anatomy Of A Horse*. This brought him to the notice of such high-born patrons as the Duke of Richmond, who commissioned three large paintings from him. Earl Spencer, ancestor of Princess Diana, also took an interest in him, as well as the Marquis of Rockingham, the Duke of Grafton, Lady Nelthorpe and eventually Laetitia, Lady Wade. The latter was a fine horsewoman who was well known for her fiery temper, foul language and indecent behaviour. Nevertheless, she and her horse made excellent subjects for an equestrian painting.

Being in demand from such wealthy clients, a move to London was essential. Stubbs and family moved to Portman Square and stayed there permanently. Although he now mixed with the aristocracy, Stubbs did not take up a deluxe lifestyle. He lived to the age of eighty-five, probably owing to the fact that he drank nothing but water and walked everywhere, thinking nothing of a 16-mile hike to visit his patrons. A self-portrait in middle age shows a healthy and confidently affluent gentleman, bewigged and elegantly dressed, in keeping with his secure standing in society.

His occupation was not, however, without its moments of danger, as well as eccentric commissions. One of his famous subjects, Whistleblower, the high-spirited colt of the Marquis of Rockingham, reared up and struck at Stubbs. Other commissions which came his way included one from Sir Joseph Banks who had travelled with Captain Cook. Banks wanted a picture of the first kangaroo ever brought to Britain. John Hunter, a surgeon, wanted portraits of a cheetah, a baboon, a rhinoceros, a moose, a macaque monkey and a yak, while 'The Lincolnshire Ox' depicts the huge bovine won in a cockfight by a John Gibbons. The creature was at least 6ft tall and weighed over 3,000lb.

As well as his superb horse and dog paintings, Stubbs was also an extremely accomplished and fashionable portrait artist. Into these pictures, Stubbs often introduced grooms and servants, making sure that all figures were treated with the same dignity and respect.

Never one to rest on his laurels and not content with only oil paint as a medium, he also researched the use of enamel paints fired into copper plates. In 1780, he contacted Josiah Wedgewood and was invited to visit the Etruria pottery. The two collaborated on the making of large plaques which became popular with the gentry.

His fitness regime served him well and he was still greatly in demand into his eighties. Having painted the Prince of Wales on horseback, he contrasted this with a series on the theme of farm workers, called 'Haymakers and Reapers'. Fine attention to authentic detail remained important to him and his final work was 'A Comparative Anatomical Exposition of the Structure of the Human Body with that of a Tiger and a Common Fowl'.

How's that for a very senior Scouser citizen?

Clive Swift

It's all Bouquets for Richard Bucket

Richard! Don't do that, dear! Richard! Watch out for that cyclist, he's only a mile away. Richard! Are you going to alarm me for my birthday?' The alarm refers to a domestic burglar alarm and Richard, is, of course, Clive Swift, playing the long-suffering husband of Hyacinth Bucket. Here is an actor who is so credible in every role he undertakes, his audiences have great difficulty in realising that he is only pretending. The slightly stooped shoulders, the bland expression and ultra-conventional style of dress seem to be the natural attributes of the man. However, take him to another studio, theatre or film-set and you will hardly recognise him. As well as joining Patricia Routledge in the vacuum of suburbia, Clive has been highly acclaimed in a variety of Shakespearian plays, in the BBC adaptation of *Barchester Towers*, in *Doctor Who*, *A Passage to India*, *Peak Practice*, *Excalibur*, *First Among Equals*, *Inspector Morse* and in his own one-man show, *Richard's Bucket Overflows*, at the Edinburgh Festival. For the latter, Clive has composed all the words and music for the entirely new set of songs included in the evening's entertainment.

Clive's journey to the refined respectability of Upper Echelon, began, appropriately enough, in Southport, where, between 1940 and 1949, he attended Croxton Preparatory School. His next visiting card was presented at Clifton College, an independent boarding school in Bristol, situated in beautiful surroundings and having its own theatre. From there, he was accepted by Gonville and Caius College, Cambridge, where he graduated with an MA (Hons) in English Literature. He recalls his days in the hallowed seat of learning with great nostalgia, although in the vacation between sixth form and university, he was a little apprehensive. 'I thought Cambridge would be a place of grim study,' is the way he puts it. But in reality it was an extremely happy experience. 'I appeared in twenty-three plays over a three-year period, alongside Derek Jacobi, Ian McKellan and many others who were destined for stardom. It proved to be my entrée into the profession. What luck!'

Leaving academia and doing his bit in the military, Clive was awarded the Cyprus Medal for peacekeeping services between the Turkish and Greek sections of Cyprus. Of course, when back in Blighty, he took every opportunity to visit the theatre. 'In 1965,' he says, 'I went to see Ken Dodd at the London Palladium. He was such a consummate performer that he immediately became a hero of mine. Many years later, he actually asked me for my autograph. I couldn't believe it! But I returned the compliment when my brother and I enjoyed that most hilarious of all shows, *An Audience With Ken Dodd*. I was delighted to ask one of the comic questions.'

Another of Clive's heroes was Lancashire County Cricket Club's Cyril Washbrook. 'I met him once, in his President's Room at Old Trafford,' he says. 'It turned out that his wife was an ardent fan of *Keeping Up Appearances*.'

The years between 1960 and 1968, while on long-term contract with the Royal Shakespeare Company, were particularly happy for Clive. As well as enjoying a miscellany of interesting roles, he felt he was so fortunate to be 'learning from the best in the land'. Having learned from the best, he then returned the favour

by passing on that knowledge, teaching young hopefuls at both LAMDA (London Academy of Music and Dramatic Art) and RADA. As a permanent follow-up to this, he wrote two guide books for budding thespians, *The Job Of Acting* and *The Performing World Of The Actor*. His help for others also includes his support for UNICEF, helping children from around the world especially in developing nations. Modestly he says, 'I do what I can for them.'

Clive is lucky enough to belong to a loyal and supportive family, with one sister, Ruth and one brother, David (see p. 121). Having, at one time, been married to the author, Margaret Drabble, their grown-up children are Adam who is a university don at Balliol College, Oxford; Becky, the director of the Literary Consultancy; and Joe, a landscape designer and television presenter. In recent years, John Moores University has added to Clive's own laurels with an Honorary Fellowship.

Although the viewing public associated Clive so strongly with the role of Richard Bucket, proof of his versatility occurred when he joined the BBC series *Born and Bred* and made the part of the vicar, the Revd Brewer, his own.

Earlier in life, he had a uniquely interesting experience. When a young actor is offered the chance to work with someone of the stature of Peter Ustinov, he doesn't turn it down, even if it is only for one day's work and it is in Skopje, in the former Yugoslavia. 'I was determined to get there,' says Clive, 'but I was off flying at that time. So I travelled all the way overland. It felt almost like a pilgrimage. But it was worth it. Peter Ustinov rewarded me by singing for me and by telling some of his hilarious anecdotes. I'll never forget him.'

Perhaps the influence of that superb raconteur has a bearing on the fact that Clive says, 'I'm keen to bring my stand-up cabaret show, *Richard's Bucket Overflows*, to Liverpool as soon as possible.' For such a special occasion there is bound to be an eager audience, especially if there will be 'light refreshments' or a 'candle-lit supper' during the interval.

David Swift

Accomplished and Witty Actor

Lights! Camera! Action! Time for the television news. The theme music plays and captions roll. The montage of news footage follows; fast, furious and topical. Sitting at the news desk, only seconds before the camera is due to focus on him, Henry Davenport, middle-aged newscaster, glances at himself in a tiny hand mirror, adjusts his toupée and takes a swig from a hip flask. His co-presenter assumes her sweetest false smile, tries to edge him off the screen and, right on cue, they deliver coverage of the day's events. With clear, precise diction, their performance is flawless and they end the programme the best of friends. Or so it would seem to the viewers at home. But the viewers at home are not at all surprised when the news is over and the bitching begins. This is 1990 and the third series of Channel Four's enormously successful, satirical situation comedy, *Drop The Dead Donkey*.

David Swift, the actor who played Henry Davenport so suavely for eight years in every episode of the hilarious comedy, was nominated for the Olivier Award for best actor and, with the rest of the cast, earned a nomination for best sitcom.

David's journey towards television took him on a varied and unusual route. When he was still a child, his family moved from their first home in Wavertree, to Allerton and later to Bootle. David and brother Clive, along with their sister Ruth, had parents who, although not professional thespians, were very talented. Mrs Swift had a gift for music and Mr Swift's personality was extremely humorous.

While still very young, David attended Beechenhurst Kindergarten, in a large Victorian house facing the main entrance to Calderstones Park. Between the ages of six and nine, his more formal education began at the Junior Section of Liverpool College. After excellent academic achievements at Clifton College, Bristol, and gaining his MA at Cambridge, David qualified as a barrister. During his twenties, however, he enrolled in a management course run by Marks & Spencer. He became one of their managers and was later invited to become a director at J.&P. Jacobs, Aintree, one of Marks & Spencer's principal clothing manufacturers.

David's undoubted literary and academic talents proved to be invaluable when he moved to London and became a reading editor at the publishers, Calder and Boyers. At the same time, he also became an author in his own right. All this before the age of thirty. It was at the suggestion of his actress wife, Paula Jacobs, and his younger brother Clive, that David decided to emulate Shakespeare's idea that, 'like a crab, you could go sideways' into a different way of life.

Quite soon, he joined the cast of a soap opera, *Couples*, starring as one of the several characters needing marriage guidance. Then came the BBC's distinguished serialisation of *War and Peace*, in which David played Napoleon. 'On location in Yugoslavia,' he recalls, 'shooting the lead up to the Battle of Austerlitz, I had to sit astride a magnificent white horse. The whole of the French army marched past to honour their general. So Napoleon, very dignified and self-important, was required to acknowledge their salute. Looking back, I have to admit I enjoyed that. Who wouldn't be tickled at a whole regiment of 3,000 soldiers looking up and saluting in unison? But here's the rub. These Napoleonic warriors were really just 300 extras, members of the Yugoslavian Territorials, kitted out in fancy uniforms. But I said 3,000, didn't I? 300! Multiplied later by technical wizardry.'

'On another occasion,' he recollects, 'I was playing Talbot in the Royal Shakespeare Company's production of *Henry VI* at the Aldwych. I had what I

thought was one of the best stage entrances of all time. A bridge is lowered onto the stage from the "flies". On the bridge, in a spotlight, stands Talbot, wearing full armour, most impressive. Until the night when the bridge stuck, hanging in mid-air, tilting sideways. A bridge too far from the stage! In full view of the audience! The seriously intellectual Shakespearian devotees rocked with laughter while I tried to make myself invisible, lying down behind the parapet. After an eternity, when the technicalities were finally corrected and the bridge plonked down onto the boards, enter Hastings, whose first line to me was, "My Lord Talbot. At last returned." It brought the house down!'

In Arnold Wesker's play, *Wedding Feast*, David was required to appear, as Litvinov, full-frontal nude, steeping into a bath. 'The character was supposed to be an overweight businessman with a heart of gold but I was so self-conscious, I trained and trimmed until I felt fit to be seen in public. My wife said I became quite vain about my body but "anno domini" soon caught up with me!' David says he particularly enjoyed his long West End run as Frank Doel in *84, Charing Cross Road* in the early 1980s. Equally, in 2000, he loved playing the eponymous Oscar in a television series for children, *Oscar Charlie*.

In conversation, David recalls some of Liverpool's regretful past. 'Many of our forebears were guilty of shameful deeds,' he says, 'but at least our generation is ready to admit how wrong this was. We are prepared to apologise and try to make amends.'

David says he feels honoured to be a trustee and executive head of a charity set up by his benevolent father-in-law. 'We recently helped to establish a Children's Gallery at the National Museums of Liverpool but we are also spreading beyond Merseyside with other activities,' he explains. 'I personally donate to the establishments that educated me, and to a number of groups helping indigenous parts of the world, and the infirm . . . and, of course the Actors' Benevolent Fund.'

David appreciates his good fortune at having a wonderful family, his wife, Paula, and daughter Julia, also an actress, son-in-law, actor David Bamber, and brother Clive. 'How sad I was to lose my young colleague, Richard Beckinsale, from our sitcom *Bloomers* when he was only thirty-one. I feel so much for his family.'

Hugh Owen Thomas 1834–91

Weird but Wonderful 'Father' of Modern Orthopaedic Surgery

It is impossible to write about either of the two illustrious doctors, Hugh Owen Thomas and Robert Jones, without describing their mutual heredity and altruistic achievements. Never were two close relatives imbued with such similar gifts but with such utterly contrasting personalities. (See p. 66)

Robert Jones, the younger of the two, was a greatly loved and highly esteemed surgeon and teacher, whose advice on the treatment of wounds and fractures in the First World War was of inestimable value to military medical officers, including Captain Noel Chavasse (see p. 16) and his colleagues. His vast knowledge and instinctive understanding of the subject came to him via a long family line of medical innovators, most notably from his uncle, Hugh Owen Thomas.

To understand fully the background of these two pioneers, we need to delve into their family history. Way back in 1745, a shipwreck near Anglesey left many dead and drowned. A Welsh farmer who was also a part-time smuggler managed to save the life of one little boy. He carried the injured child home to his wife and they brought him up as their own. They had no idea where the ship had come from and could only guess at the boy's strange-sounding native language. They thought it might possibly be Spanish. The boy learned quickly and was grateful to his foster parents. He helped to tend their livestock on the farm. To everyone's surprise he quickly displayed an inborn talent for nursing any sick or injured animals, even attending to damaged limbs and open wounds. Untutored though he was, when he grew up all the local farmers came to rely upon his veterinary skills. In time, mothers began to bring their children to him after any accidents. Farm workers and fisherman trusted him with fractures, dislocations or joint pains. When he married, his own sons showed the same instinctive talents. As well as farming and rearing sheep, this family became accepted as the local bone-setters and healers of all ailments. As time went by, the family's unorthodox medical skills were passed down from father to son and then to grandson.

In 1834, when one of these grandsons, Evan Thomas, was nineteen, he left the hills and valleys of Wales to settle in Liverpool. His cures were eagerly accepted by the dock workers and sailors but, of course, not every case was successful. Some of the most serious cases were already beyond help. The long-established and fully qualified doctors of the city labelled this upstart a quack and a charlatan. 'Docker turned doctor' was only one of their jibes. On at least three occasions, he was hauled before the justices and accused of manslaughter. His Celtic eloquence convinced the court that these poor souls were already at death's door long before he was called. Malpractice was never proved and he walked free each time.

Evan Thomas was determined that these undeserved allegations should never be repeated. When he married and had five sons, he made sure they all qualified at the

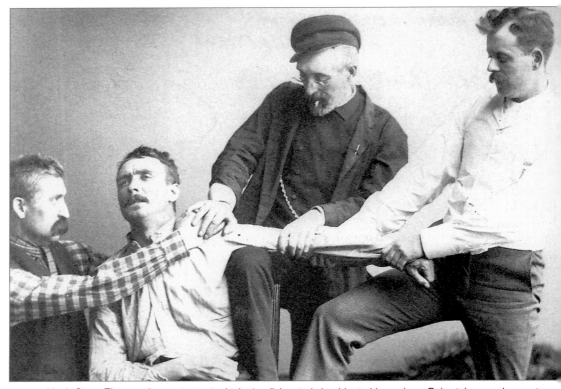

Hugh Owen Thomas demonstrates 'reducing' a dislocated shoulder to his nephew, Robert Jones, who went on to become a highly respected orthopaedic surgeon.

finest medical establishments of the time. Each one trained at Edinburgh University and all became bona fide doctors. Because he was so proud to have fathered such a dynasty of genuine medical practitioners, he paid to have excellent portraits painted of each of them. They were his personal status symbols.

The eldest, Hugh Owen Thomas, had already spent a probationary four years helping his uncle, a conventionally qualified doctor in North Wales. After four years at Edinburgh and a further two at University College London, Hugh was accepted as a member of the Royal College of Surgeons.

In 1857, young Hugh returned to Liverpool and joined his father to work with the many sick and poor around the dockland area. But Hugh soon began to show signs of a brusque and outspoken character. His criticism irked his father. Both had eccentric streaks in their personalities and the liaison soon ended.

Hugh Owen Thomas was all brain and brilliant ideas but had no social skills at all. He never worked in a hospital, couldn't fit in with his father's ways and began to display some very idiosyncratic behaviour. Despite his excellent degrees, he had no interest in private practice. Surprisingly, he managed to find himself a very pretty wife, as her portrait in the Liverpool Medical Institute testifies. They were married in 1864. Instead of settling in Rodney Street where all the leading specialists had their consulting rooms, Hugh chose a rambling place in Nelson Street, near the dock area. Here, he set up his own version of a clinic. Although he had no charm and definitely no bedside manner, his reputation as a healer spread like warm ointment over a grazed knee. Patients flocked to his surgery. There were so many queues, he had to treat his consulting room like a production line. Cubicles were erected so that he could move rapidly from one undressed patient to the next.

Treatment very often resembled torture. Without anaesthetics, he would frequently use the techniques of a chiropractor, jolting joints back into place with the violent force of his hands, or rushing at people from behind, taking them by surprise and snapping bones that had already been wrongly set by incompetent colleagues. Some slanderers tried to claim that he was breaking good bones so that he could experiment on them.

It wasn't only his unorthodox medical practices that created this love-hate relationship with patients. Rapidly, his appearance changed from the normal looking young man in his early portrait. His mode of dress marked him as an eccentric almost to the point of weirdness. He always wore the same, dark, high-buttoned jacket, a sailor's cap pulled down over one defective eye, and gauntlet gloves. A cigarette constantly dangled from his lips, whether diagnosing, operating or visiting patients.

He was a man of great contradictions. Despite his strength, he was tiny and frail-looking, darting about and appearing suddenly from nowhere. He was addicted to tobacco, worked himself to a shadow, yet preached fresh air and prolonged rest for his patients.

He never took a day off. When he called Sunday his free day he didn't mean it was his day of rest. He meant all consultations on that day were free for the really poor. He had no time for church, chapel nor religion of any sort. In fact, he became an agnostic. Sunday was his busiest day with a waiting room that overflowed into the street. Elizabeth, his beautiful and religious wife seemed content with this. He never went out for pleasure. He had no hobbies nor interests beyond medicine. His only forays into the outside world were visits to housebound patients, always the poor, never the wealthy. To get about he raced through the streets of Liverpool in a strange little cart with bright red wheels, pulled by two black horses.

His previous connections with rural Wales were useful. At the back of his premises, he employed a blacksmith and a saddler to make the splints that he invented. After being correctly set, broken limbs had to be kept immobile until the fracture had healed. By means of these splints, patients were then able to walk, as long as the leg was held straight between iron rods. These were kept in place by wide leather straps, usually shaped to cover the knee.

This so-called 'Thomas Splint' was subsequently responsible for saving the lives of many combatants with shattered limbs during both world wars.

As he was a general practitioner as well as an orthopaedic expert, he treated all manner of ailments. Intestinal obstructions were another of his special interests. Tuberculosis was rife at the time and he became an authority on that, too. He again insisted on fresh air and plenty of rest.

But he never rested. He darted about like a manic firecracker. His workload became heavier with each passing year and he welcomed it. Without x-rays, instinct and meticulous investigation were essential and in these areas he surpassed his rivals. By this time, his fifteen-year-old nephew Robert Jones had come to live with him. In any other occupation, the next few years would be called an apprenticeship but both uncle and nephew regarded it more highly than that. Even after he qualified, young Robert was keen to return to Nelson Street. Photographs show the two men treating fractures and deformities together, Hugh always with his ever-present cigarette drooping from his lips. Hugh Owen Thomas's inspired designs for splints produced such obvious results that the public, if not his detractors, acknowledged his unique abilities. His brusque, almost rude manner became part of his persona, drawing patients to him rather than repelling them.

During the Franco-Prussian War, Thomas offered his splints to the French military but he was rebuffed. Young Robert, however, could understand the tremendous advantages of these appliances. He was determined to build on the knowledge he was gaining at his uncle's energetic elbow.

Hugh Owen Thomas abhorred inefficiency or neglect. He commanded relatives of patients to carry out his instructions to the last detail. But his self-neglect was obvious. His own health deteriorated. Photographs taken shortly before his death, at the early age of fifty-seven, show a man who looked at least eighty. At his funeral in Toxteth, working-class and poverty-stricken ex-patients and their families far outnumbered the hierarchy of the medical profession.

His epitaph consists of the exceptional career of Sir Robert Jones, the nephew whom Hugh Owen Thomas had so successfully trained.

Ricky Tomlinson

A Man of Many Parts with a very Special Heart

William Shakespeare could almost have been thinking of Ricky Tomlinson when he wrote: 'One man in his time plays many parts.' Here is a man who has never had an acting lesson in his life and yet is in constant demand for more and more character parts. He has won so many awards that he has lost count of the actual number. Among them are various BAFTA nominations and prizes, the Royal Television Society Comedy Award, the Liverpool Personality Award and an award from BBC Radio Merseyside. The biggest surprise of his life was winning the Comedy Performance of the Year in competition with Jimmy Nesbitt and Paul Whitehouse, two actors for whom he has the highest admiration.

These days, Ricky's fame, like Jim Royle's beer belly, has spread far and wide. Back in his childhood days in Everton, when young Ricky was a pupil at Heyworth Street and then at Venice Street Primary Schools, he used to love going to the local library near St George's Church. On Saturdays, he'd go with his mates to the Everton Picture Palace. His imagination was fired by such children's classics as *Treasure Island* and *Black Beauty*, and he used to write his own little stories and poems in secret. In secret because his mates didn't consider that sort of thing to be very macho. As well as school, once a week Ricky had to attend Myrtle Street Children's Hospital for injections to alleviate his asthma attacks, so that he could join his pals playing football.

Ricky's parents were always supportive and had hearts of gold. His father's bakery was also in Heyworth Street where the hours were long and hard. Being a baker in the Second World War was a reserved occupation essential to the whole community. Whatever bombs were being dropped, everyone still needed their staple diet of bread. Even when the sirens wailed out their warnings of yet another attack and everyone else rushed for the air-raid shelters, Ricky's father kept on kneading the dough and baking the crusty loaves, regardless of his own safety. Ricky's beloved Mam was just as hardworking. At various times she did domestic cleaning, worked in a laundry and in a factory, all the while bringing up her family of boys and looking after the home, in the most loving and dedicated way.

During his teenage years, Ricky studied at Walton Technical College and passed his City and Guilds exams. He is a qualified plasterer and can turn his hand to any number of DIY jobs. These came in handy when renovating his parents' house and, later, his own club and the offices of his own theatrical agency where he and his brother provided work for hundreds of film and television extras.

He has also been a salesman and once had a stall in Great Homer Street Market, close to the stall of Cilla Black's mother. To attract custom, Ricky used his musical talents and his natural sense of humour. He would sometimes serenade passers-by on his banjo. At other times he would put up a notice by the large puddle at the side of his stall. The sign said 'NO FISHING'.

Ricky with patients and their parents at Ronald McDonald House in Alder Hey Hospital.

As time went by, Ricky found himself drawn to comedy clubs and folk clubs in the Merseyside area, including the Fur and Feathers Social Club. While acting as compère, introducing the variety and musical acts, he couldn't resist throwing in a few gags of his own. Things just developed naturally from there. Without realising it, he was becoming a stand-up comedian at the same time as working in the building trade.

This gift for ad-libbing brought him, almost by chance, into the world of television. Not being a professional 'luvvie', one early experience took him by surprise. After answering an advert for people with Trade Union experience, he received a phone call booking him to do a workshop in Oldham for a director named Roland Joffe. Proud of his City and Guilds qualifications, Ricky loaded all his tools into his van and set off. What the naïve young Ricky didn't realise, at the time, was that 'a workshop' in show business means improvising scenes on a given theme to let a director or casting director see your strengths in characterisation. It took a while to sink in but it was smiles all round when Ricky got the job. The play, *United Kingdom*, was transmitted by the BBC to great critical praise and Ricky's future as a professional actor was assured.

On one occasion, filming outside Liverpool Town Hall, which doubled for the palace of the Tsar of Russia, the crowd was supposed to be baying for the blood of the unpopular Russian leader. The director came to Ricky and the other extras, complimented them on their rough and ready shouts and jeers. 'That was great,' he said, 'but could you shout "Death to the Tsar!" instead of "Come down here and I'll knock yer bloody block off, yer bastid!"' Since then Ricky has played major roles in so many films and television programmes that the complete list would fill this book. A favourite period of his career was performing in two of Ken Loach's movies. Ricky was nominated for Best Supporting Actor for his role in *Riff Raff* at the Berlin Film Festival; the film itself won Best Picture.

Among his other credits are *Boys From The Black Stuff*; *The Virgin Of Liverpool*; *Mike Basset, England Manager*; *Cracker*; *Hillsborough*; *The 51st State*; *Nice Guy Eddie*, a series of adverts for British Gas and the two long-running series for which he is best known, first as Bobby Grant in *Brookside*, and then as Jim Royle in *The Royle Family*. In both of these he was 'married' to Sue Johnston, as both Sheila Grant and Barbara Royle. In real life, he has also been married twice, originally to Marlene, the mother of their children, and now to Rita.

Ricky says that audiences assume that he is 100 per cent like couch potato, Jim Royle. 'But that's not right,' he protests, 'I'm only 95 per cent like him!' He certainly got out of his armchair long enough to work hard on Liverpool's successful bid to become the European Capital of Culture in 2008. Ricky has a strong sense of justice and has embraced many causes in his time. These have often landed him in hot water but he has also done indefatigable work in his countless charity appearances.

In 2006, Ricky was joined by comedienne Jo Brand, as contestants on *Who Wants To Be A Millionaire?* They won the princely sum of £64,000 on behalf of Ronald McDonald House at Alder Hey Children's Hospital in West Derby. Alder Hey is the largest children's hospital in Europe and Ronald McDonald House provides residential facilities for the parents and siblings of seriously ill patients who constantly need their families near them. 'We have so much to thank Ricky for,' says Jan Thomas, of the charity. 'No one can ever know what a superb help he has been to us.'

Open-heart surgery for a quadruple bypass in 2008 did not prevent Ricky from working tirelessly for the Capital of Culture celebrations and for many local charities.

Cathy Tyson

Cold, Secretive Simone . . .
Warm, Candid Cathy

The Dingle area of Liverpool is Cathy's childhood home and the Everyman Theatre is her alma mater. But the world is her oyster. The daughter of a barrister from Trinidad and an English social worker, young Cathy attended St Finbar's Primary School in South Hill Street, Our Lady of Mount Carmel in North Hill Street and then St Winifred's in Park Street. It was at the age of seventeen that Cathy decided to leave formal education, earn a little ready cash by working on a market stall and then join the Everyman Youth Theatre.

This brought her into the very heart of Liverpool's cultural community. The theatre is close to the city's main university (it has three), as well as the Philharmonic Concert Hall, the art college and the ex-Institute School for Boys, now Sir Paul McCartney's Liverpool Institute for the Performing Arts. As the Everyman is situated on Hope Street, it is halfway between the two great cathedrals.

Less than a stone's throw away, Canning Street, the red light district of the time, was home to the city's many prostitutes. By coincidence, it was Cathy's first major role as Simone, a slender, stylish and secretive prostitute, that led to instant fame and acclaim for the beautiful Liverpudlian. She had already played a variety of roles at the Everyman and at Theatr Clwyd in North Wales, and had won admission to the Royal Shakespeare Company. But playing Simone, the love interest for Bob Hoskins in the film *Mona Lisa*, immediately brought her a BAFTA nomination, the Seattle Golden Globe Award and the Los Angeles Film Critics' Award.

It was in about 1987, when I [the author] was about to enter a fashion boutique in Church Street in Liverpool city centre. I was approached by a group of shop assistants who politely requested me to boycott the shop as they were all on strike. They were out in support of the manageress who had been sacked for upholding a complaint about sexual harassment experienced by one of the younger employees. Naturally, I agreed with their sentiments and immediately went elsewhere, little realising that this would subsequently become the subject of a film starring Cathy Tyson, Glenda Jackson and John Thaw. The film, called *Business As Usual*, won great critical acclaim and would be worthy of a repeat showing.

A short marriage of five years to *Coronation Street* and *Red Dwarf* actor Craig Charles brought them a son, Jack, to whom Cathy is so very grateful for all the countless hours he has spent with her. She says, 'Jack has always been supportive of my career, always wanting me to do a good job, always wanting me to aim high. What's more, he never complains about me going round the house talking in strange accents!' Perhaps the strange accents are practice for her work as a voice-over artist! Cathy is also extremely proud of her mother, Margaret, a dedicated social worker who 'always has a great sense of hope about her'. Cathy adds, 'My

Mum was a single parent in the '70s when there was still an air of shame about it. But she never allowed it to trouble her. In fact she has been my constant support, always with me and always "there" for me. In my eyes, she ought to be made a dame!'

In 1998, Cathy was cast as Cleopatra in the English Shakespeare Company's production of *Antony and Cleopatra*. She also took leading roles in the Royal Shakespeare Company's open air productions in Regent Park.

Her career brought her opportunities not given to many. She filmed *The Serpent and the Rainbow* in Haiti, playing a psychiatrist. She says, 'I remember watching voodoo dancers possessed by spirits. It was frightening. They were so careless of their own safety. I found it very disturbing. Funnily enough, the only thing that got me through was thinking of Liverpool.'

She has also filmed in the rainforests of French Guyana. When her scenes were completed and it was time for her to leave, there were tears in the eyes of the director. 'I was touched by that,' says Cathy. Appearing in Barbara Taylor-Bradford's *Remember* brought her another interesting opportunity, working in America. Her most controversial role was as the housekeeper having an affair with an ordained clergyman, in *Priest*.

One of the favourite periods in her career was working on the television series *Band of Gold* between 1995 and 1997, written by Kay Mellor. Once again, Cathy played a prostitute. 'That character was one of my best parts,' she recalls. Actors become accustomed to odd experiences. One of Cathy's occurred early in her career, when understudying actor Jim Hooper. 'On the very first night of a show called *Red Roses*, he got his foot caught in the trap door, centre stage,' she remembers. 'I'll never forget his scream! I had to go on instead of him, as the character Bells. No lines to say, just ringing bells attached to my costume. Most peculiar! But I did get to perform alongside Anthony Sher, who was very kind. I felt like a hero helping to save the show.'

In contrast to the 'hard as nails' character, the aloof and enigmatic prostitute, Simone, Cathy is really very vulnerable and emotional. She recently received an award from the *Manchester Evening News* 'And I wept buckets,' she says, 'in front of a 300-strong audience. Very embarrassing. I just couldn't stop.'

In 2006, Cathy received a request to play the part of Condoleezza Rice at the Liverpool Philharmonic Hall. She turned this down but reported that instead she would be joining the protestors outside the hall, in Hope Street. 2007 was a year for interesting roles. Firstly as Miss Gayle, the deputy head of *Grange Hill*, then a guest appearance in *Emmerdale*. In December, 2007, Cathy played Herodia, in the modern version of the *Liverpool Nativity*, directed by Liverpool actress/director Noreen Kershaw. Cathy's musical portrayal of the embittered, scheming head of state, dramatically dancing across the famous mosaic floor of St George's Hall, won her universal praise.

In reality she has a high regard for the charity AddAction. 'It's marvellous. It does a lot of painstaking work with addicts, helping them to come off substances. Society views these people as time-wasters but the charity doesn't. It cares.' She also hosts events for the Sick Children's Trust as well as supporting other charities.

Now that her home city is happily experiencing such an uplifting decade, Cathy wants to send her warmest wishes, 'For a memorable 2008 and beyond,' adding, 'I've never stopped loving Liverpool, although because of work, I've been away for a while.'

Kitty Wilkinson 1786–1860
Cleanliness and Godliness

If ever the expression 'Cleanliness is next to Godliness' applied to any one person in particular, it must certainly have been to Kitty Wilkinson, a working-class girl with natural common sense, a practical understanding of the importance of hygiene and an extremely caring personality. Her name and fame have become synonymous with saintly devotion to others and her achievements are now legendary – to the extent that she is commemorated by a stained-glass window in Liverpool's Anglican Cathedral.

Kitty's life was blighted by tragedy from a very early age. She was born in Londonderry, in either 1785 or 1786, to an Irish mother and an English father, with the family name spelled either Seaward or Seward. So Catherine Seward was how the intelligent and warm-hearted little girl was originally known.

There are varying opinions as to the date and cause of her father's early death. Some say he died of natural causes in Ireland, others that he brought Kitty to Liverpool and that Mrs Seward died on the journey across the Irish Sea, leaving the young widower free to marry again. Thus, Kitty had a step-mother who turned out to have severe mental problems. But a more likely version is that, on the family's voyage to Merseyside in 1794, when a violent storm suddenly battered their ship, he was swept overboard and perished almost in sight of their destination. What is almost certain is that there was a storm and that the baby of the family was wrenched from Mr Seward's arms by a gigantic wave and there was absolutely nothing that could be done to save it. In most accounts, Mr Seward never arrived in Liverpool.

Somehow, Kitty, her little brother and their mother survived but the shock had a terrible and permanent effect on Mrs Seward's physical and mental health. From then on she suffered from bouts of depression and instability and her sight gradually deteriorated. Her eventual loss of sight was a serious blow because she had once been a gifted lace-maker, able to teach others the skill.

So, fatherless at the age of nine, Kitty had to help her doubly bereaved mother to find somewhere to live in this unknown town. They managed to settle in a cellar in Denison Street and then find domestic work with a Mrs Lightbody, possibly taking the little brother with them each day. Mrs Lightbody was a kind and generous woman. In spite of her own failing sight, she encouraged Kitty to improve her reading and writing skills and to develop strong beliefs concerning duty and service to others.

After two years, Mrs Seward's health worsened, so much so that she was taken into the Liverpool Infirmary. Later she returned to Ireland to be cared for by her own family. This left the eleven-year-old Kitty and her little brother entirely without parental protection. Mrs Lightbody thought she was doing them a favour by sending them to work in a cotton mill in Caton, Lancashire. But the work was hard

and the hours unbelievably long. There is no further mention of the young boy. It is possible that he couldn't survive the exploitation, poor nourishment and harsh conditions of the times.

Eventually, news arrived that Mrs Lightbody had died and that Mrs Seward had returned to Liverpool. Kitty escaped from the mill to look after her mother and was fortunate enough to find work with a Colonel and Mrs Maxwell who treated her well and allowed her to join the local Unitarian church. But just less than a year later, the Maxwells decided to leave Liverpool. They invited Kitty to join them in their new home but she felt that she couldn't leave her ailing mother.

Instead she changed employers to clean and scrub in a Mrs Heywood's household. At the same time, she was always more than willing to help others worse off than herself.

As the years went by, it became impossible to leave Mrs Seward alone. She needed constant attention. Kitty searched and found a place where she and her mother could live together and Kitty could use part of the premises as a school room to teach local children. Obviously, her studies in Mrs Lightbody's house had been useful. Kitty would probably have become a talented, though untrained teacher. The trouble was, Mrs Seward's behaviour was now dangerously out of control. Her fits of violent aggression scared Kitty's pupils. She often set fire to things for no reason at all. She was mentally far beyond giving any instruction in her previous skills of spinning and lace-making. Kitty was reduced to doing such soul-destroying jobs as collecting horse-manure during the hours of darkness, to sell for fertiliser to farmers and gardeners. She still took any cleaning jobs she could find. In spite of everything, she was cheerful and helpful to everyone.

When Kitty was twenty-seven, she met and fell in love with a young Frenchman named Emmanuel De Monte. He might have been a French Canadian sailor or an ex-prisoner of war who had stayed on in Liverpool. There is no certainty of this. But it is certain that he and Kitty were married in St Peter's church, in 1812 and that they had a son in 1813.

About three years later, De Monte left for Canada, possibly with the idea of emigrating with his wife and child to French-speaking Montreal. Soon after he left, Kitty realised that she was pregnant again. But the cruel sea was to deal her another blow, wrecking the outward-bound ship, and killing her husband just as it had killed her father many years earlier. Now Kitty and her mother were both widows.

The difficult birth of her second child took its toll on Kitty's already weakened health. But she still had to go out to work, this time for a pittance in a nail factory, where her hands were badly damaged by the molten metal. She still went charring from time to time and was highly regarded for her tender nursing skills. When one of her elderly employers died, the lady's widower donated a mangle to Kitty as a thank-you gift for caring for the long suffering Mrs Braik. Therefore, Kitty added laundering to her many part-time jobs.

For ten years, Kitty continued to support her two sons and her more than difficult mother. Then, at the age of thirty-eight, well into middle-age in those days, she met Thomas Wilkinson, who worked in William Rathbone's warehouse. Kitty was nine years older than Thomas, and no beauty, but Wilkinson, also a Unitarian, was happy to take on responsibility for the whole family. Kitty and Thomas were married in 1823. For a while, Wilkinson's small but regular wage helped them to live frugally but reasonably well. The two were devoted to each other and became friendly with some of the more educated people of the area, thus lifting their social status a little. Kitty was still helping the less fortunate at every opportunity.

It was nine years later that she and her second husband were really tested to the limits of human endurance. In 1832, a terrible plague of cholera broke out in Liverpool. It spread rapidly among the poverty stricken families living in cramped conditions, huddled together in cellars, without the benefit of running water and in premises with only one outdoor lavatory to serve up to ten families.

Thousands of people were suffering from the symptoms of fever, sickness and diarrhoea, followed often by coma or even death. At that time, no one was sure how the illness was spread. Was it by touch, breath or even by extreme panic at the very thought of being in contact with a victim? Some people collapsed with anxiety. Certainly, many doctors, priests and undertakers refused to go into infected dwellings for fear of carrying the plague to their own families or parishioners. Instinctively, Kitty felt that the soiled clothes and the tattered bed-linen of the beleaguered families were a health hazard. Her current home had water laid on. Some years before, she had managed to add a water boiler to her washing equipment. So now she invited as many people as possible to bring their laundry to be washed and disinfected with a weak solution of chloride of lime. She also warned that all clothing should be fully aired before use, preferably in the open air. Her natural intuition was right and resulted in some improvement. Exhausted though she was, by helping the mothers and grandmothers, she indirectly helped hundreds of children and adults to minimise the risks of infection. But she wished she had more than one kitchen, boiler and mangle so that her work could spread to a far wider community.

Thomas helped her unstintingly. Between them, they fostered orphans and fed the needy with gruel and milk. They gave away most of their own bedding and eventually persuaded the District Provident Society to donate more bedding and cast-off clothing from richer families to the poor. Even if, at that time, there had been any laws or regulations about adopting, teaching or administering medicines without qualifications, it is obvious that Kitty would have flouted these rules, believing that a higher authority was prompting her to do everything in her power to alleviate suffering and bring health education to as many victims as possible.

Grief had never been far away from Kitty's own life. As well as the death of her mother, Kitty now had to bear the loss of her youngest son. Her eldest son, John, had already moved away from Liverpool.

Gradually, people outside the Wilkinsons' own neighbourhood began to hear about this woman's heroic efforts. In particular, Thomas's employer, William Rathbone, had always taken a fatherly interest in his workman and now funds began to trickle through, possibly contributed anonymously by the Rathbone family. It was not until fourteen years later, however, that the corporation opened the first public baths and wash-house. Even so, they were in the forefront of innovative thought at that time. Liverpool had the first ever municipal wash-house in the whole of Britain. And who more fitted to be the salaried superintendents than Kitty and her loyal husband? Of course, they were delighted to be so honoured and, as ever, worked long and hard to maintain good standards. Just as in ancient times around the village pond or local stream, the wash-house became a place of social gatherings for wives, mothers and grandmothers.

Liverpool was beginning to wake up to the fact that efforts had to be made to improve health and living conditions. The Rathbone family was taking increasing interest in the wonderful work done by the Wilkinsons. Kitty was introduced to the Lady Mayoress and to other gentlewomen of standing in the city. Her reputation was growing apace. So much so that in 1846, Kitty and Thomas were invited to a 'do' at Carnatic Hall, Woolton (now the site of the university halls of residence). It turned out to be the equivalent of a modern 'surprise party'. Not only was the occasion especially in honour of Kitty's achievements, but there was also a presentation of a silver tea service, by none other than Queen Victoria herself. Kitty was thrilled with the inscription, 'The Queen, The Queen Dowager and the ladies of Liverpool to Catherine Wilkinson 1846'.

Further improvements were being made at the wash-house, thanks to the candle of example that Kitty had lit so many years before. Kitty and Thomas worked devotedly together for two more years until sadness once more entered Kitty's life. Just as the year 1850 was about to creep in, a severe attack of bronchitis stole Thomas's life away and with it Kitty's main source of happiness. Once again, Kitty had become a widow.

Some compensation was afforded by the fact that Kitty's son, John De Monte, returned to help her run the wash-house for twelve more years. When she eventually retired, without a formal pension, her lady sponsors made a voluntary collection to buy an annuity for her.

According to her headstone in St James' Cemetery, Catherine Wilkinson was laid to rest in November 1860, at the age of seventy-three. The reality is that this legendary little woman lives on in the improvements she inspired for the welfare of subsequent generations of Liverpudlians and in the hearts and minds of the thousands of modern-day Scousers who honour the saintly name of Kitty Wilkinson.

Joseph Williamson 1769–1840
The Mole of Edge Hill

Liverpool has many large and beautiful parks and recreation areas. One of these, officially named Wavertree Playground, is known locally as the Mystery. Nobody knows why it is called the Mystery. It's a mystery. That's why it is called the Mystery! However, 2 or 3 miles down the road towards the city centre there is an even greater mystery. A complete and utter enigma. It is a folly created by the Mole of Edge Hill.

Now a folly is defined as a structure that has no purpose other than to be there! And the Mole of Edge Hill, or the King of Edge Hill as he was also known, was Joseph Williamson. He arrived in Liverpool in 1780, at the tender age of eleven, carrying only a little tin case of clothes, and a small amount of money. He also had some good advice from his mother about making the most of his opportunities. She was back home in Warrington, 20 miles away. How he made the journey and how he immediately found a middle-class occupation is another puzzle. But he walked straight into a thriving business and pleasant lodgings with a wealthy tobacco merchant, Thomas Tate.

Young Joseph was an intelligent and willing apprentice. The dealings and accounts of the tobacco company proved to be no problem for him and he soon rose to a position of trust within the firm. So much so that in 1802 Joseph married Thomas Tate's daughter, Elizabeth. Poor girl, she didn't know what she was letting herself in for! Certainly it wasn't much of a love match. More like a business move on the part of Joseph. In less than a year, upon the death of Elizabeth's father, he had inherited the company. Tate had already been ill at the time of the wedding. The marriage was not at all happy. There were no children. Even on the wedding day Joseph's incipient eccentricity began to show itself. Straight after the ceremony, off he went to go hunting with the local dignitaries, leaving Elizabeth to return home alone. No reception, no celebration, no loving kisses.

It was well-known that there were frequent noisy rows. Once, in a fit of spite, Joseph set free all the exotic birds from his wife's private aviary. He blamed her for their problems but it is obvious that all the troubles stemmed from his freakish personality. He quarrelled with colleagues, he was rude to his tenants and he was certainly an obsessive megalomaniac, making enormous sums of money from tobacco imports and also from property development and building.

So why are the people of Liverpool so fascinated by him? Why is he so highly regarded? Why are monuments and heritage centres being created to commemorate him? The answer is that he was also kind, charming and a great social benefactor. Yes, these were the weird contradictions in this man's personality. He made friends with clergymen, town councillors, George Stephenson, the Prince of Wales (later George IV) and the poor of the area.

While he was making his fortune, something else deep inside him was driving him on. A secret obsession was burrowing away in his psyche. People with vast amounts of money can afford to indulge their whims or obsessions. With Imelda Marcos it was shoes. With Howard Hughes it was his fear of infection. With Joseph Williamson it was a desire to excavate. He was a burrower and, like 'the Borrowers', he wanted to spend his time below the dwellings of other people. More than a century before The Beatles made the Cavern world famous, this man was already beetling away, creating sandstone caverns of gigantic proportions.

No one has yet discovered what Williamson's real motivation was but he eventually owned dozens of these enormous subterranean cul-de-sac passageways.

Because this was the Edge Hill district, some tunnels had to come to an abrupt end when they reached the point where Stephenson's men were digging out tacks to carry the rail line from Manchester to Liverpool's main city station at Lime Street. The process started above ground, when Joseph constructed some arches to support decorative gardens at the rear of his own home and some other houses nearby.

Apparently, the next step came when he dug a pit under the cellar of his house in Mason Street. What strange desires this set off inside his mind no one, not even his wife, ever understood. But the whole idea became moreish to him. As well as doing the digging himself, he began to employ others. He just wanted more and more tunnels, stone staircases and grottoes. They didn't have to lead anywhere. They didn't need any purpose. They just had to be excavated. His workforce was drawn from the local unemployed; in particular ex-soldiers from the Napoleonic Wars who had no pension nor means of support for their families. The whole hole could have been a ruse to provide wages for these deserving poor and to keep them active without it appearing to be charity. The first ever job-creation scheme, in fact.

This is the only theory that anyone has ever been able to suggest for all these subterranean chambers. They weren't catacombs. No dead were ever buried there. No treasure was ever hidden there. Bomb shelters were not needed on those days. Labyrinthine though they are, no mention was ever made of any minotaur materialising. However, on one occasion, when George Stephenson's labourers were delving into the sandstone bedrock, part of the sub-soil collapsed under them. Beneath, they were horrified to see blackened and mud-spattered creatures such as those H.G. Wells would later describe as 'Morlocks'. To the untutored men of 1829, the shock was terrifying. They thought they had dug right through to Hell. Down below, Williamson's men thought they had been caught in an avalanche. Picks and spades clattered onto the rock-bed. Every man turned tail and ran. Of course the tales of disaster later recounted to their families and friends grew wilder with every telling.

As time went by, Williamson spent more time underground than at home. In any case, his own home was most peculiar. It had passages that led nowhere. It had interior windows that only looked into the next room. One large room had no window at all. At one time, he knocked down the wall of his own sitting room and donated that room to the semi-detached house next door, to a lady who needed a playroom for her many children. Goodness knows what his wife felt about that.

Not only do these yawning caves serve no useful purpose, Williamson paid his quarrymen to trundle their blue-painted wheelbarrows full of rubble and soil out into the daylight. He then paid them to wheel it all back in again. Thousands of man-hours were spent on useless tasks, undermining the foundations of the houses above. Sometimes floors collapsed. Sometimes tenants made their own little gaps to use as rubbish chutes and private sewage drainage.

Williamson was a religious man, sometimes generous and sociable too, but always idiosyncratic. One of the tunnels led from his own house to a nearby church. But he never attended that church. He and his wife went to a church in the opposite direction. Did he feel in need of a private crypt? Although one huge grotto is known as the banqueting hall, it was to his own home that he invited a large group of important acquaintances. In a sort of kitchen area, he provided only a rough work table with cheap pots and cutlery. The food was a typical working-class dish of beans with a little bacon. Some of the dignitaries were affronted at the millionaire's apparent penny-pinching. They made their excuses and left. Those who remained were then led to a far superior room and treated to a menu fit for a king. Williamson was highly amused to have discovered who his true friends were.

In recent years the tunnels have been opened to the public. Conducted tours take place daily and a café has been created near the entrance. The hollow echoing chambers provide excellent acoustics for barber shop quartets and the café can be booked for private celebrations. The Mole would be delighted to know that his tunnels have at last proved useful to the district of Edge Hill.

Harold Wilson 1916–95

Prime Minister and MP for Huyton

When Harold Wilson was a young boy on a Scouts' outing, he inadvertently saved the life of one of his pals by knocking over a glass of milk.

Christened James Harold Wilson, the future prime minister was born in Milnbridge, just outside Huddersfield. He had one elder sister who always 'bossed him around', even into adulthood. From a very early age he showed great intellect and curiosity. Like all children, he would ask unanswerable questions such as 'When will the moon be mended?' and, aged six, 'Please can I have the *Playboy Annual* for Christmas?' Perhaps the *Playboy Annual* was different in those days!

He didn't like his primary school, mainly because of the unpleasant teacher there, although his amazing memory marked him out as the brightest pupil. At the age of six, he was already a Gilbert and Sullivan fan and could recite all the lyrics of *The Pirates of Penzance*. Harold loved the construction toy, Meccano. He once tried to construct the Sydney Harbour Bridge but ran out of pieces, so had to settle for the Forth Bridge instead. At the age of seven, while in hospital for an appendix operation, he read through the encyclopaedia and discovered an enduring love for history.

The family was politically minded, their hero being Gladstone. Although little Harold was a keen football supporter, the picture on his bedroom was a full-length portrait of William Gladstone. Harold's parents were kind, considerate and full of fun. His father, a congregationalist by religion, was a Rover Leader and his mother was Girl Guide Captain with a great joie de vivre and a ready laugh. It was natural for Harold to join the Cubs and later the Boy Scouts. On one occasion, on a camping trip with the Scouts, the milk supplied to the troop was contaminated. All but one of the thirteen boys drank the milk and went down with typhoid. The only boy who didn't drink it was spared this dreadful illness. This was because Harold had accidentally knocked over his glass, spilling all the contents. Harold, himself, became desperately ill, was rushed to hospital with the others and nearly died. Indeed, six of the boys did die. This frightening and grievous experience was never forgotten by any of the family.

Harold's secondary school was Royd's Hall but he changed to Wirral Grammar School, Bebington, situated half-way between Liverpool and Chester, when the family moved to live on the Wirral. As with many youngsters, his early ambitions were unrealistic, including undertaker, poet laureate and civil engineer.

As well as studying hard, gaining extremely high marks at school and becoming head boy, he had plenty of hobbies and time for at least one teenage sweetheart. This friendship didn't last. Harold felt that other boys were trying to discourage his girlfriend from going out with him. However, one broken romance didn't put him off girls for long. When he was in the sixth form, he happened to pass a local tennis club, where a pretty young player caught his attention. Love at first sight was certainly true for teenage Harold. He was smitten, quickly found out that her name was Gladys Mary Baldwin, hurriedly applied for membership of the club, bought a tennis racquet, got to know the object of his admiration and, within three weeks told her he was going to marry her and become Prime Minister. She took both statements with a pinch of salt but was delighted when both eventually became true.

Before either of his ambitions could be realised, Harold needed to complete his education. In 1934, he won an open exhibition to Jesus College, Oxford, to study Modern History. The sum of £60 was supplemented by Wirral County Education Committee. Mary and Harold were now separated by his studies. Their special tune was 'I'll See You Again'. Mary gave up her chance to go to university because her father couldn't meet the costs. Instead she trained as a shorthand typist and worked in the offices of Lever Brothers' soap factory in Port Sunlight. (See p. 78).

Harold proved to be a brilliant and dedicated undergraduate, gaining exceptionally high grades. Although he was always extremely short of money, Harold refused to follow the undergraduate trend of running up huge bills everywhere in Oxford. He steered clear of booze and cigarettes, was grateful for his mother's food parcels, preferred tinned salmon to fresh and added a dash of flavour to very plain cooking with his favourite HP sauce – HP of course standing for Houses of Parliament. When he did mix with the 'in crowd', he impressed everyone with his remarkable perspicacity and logic. He soon became one of the finest scholars of his generation. When he decided to change his studies from History to Philosophy, Politics and Economics, he found that he needed to learn German first. In six weeks he had mastered this new language.

Following his graduation he was awarded the George Webb Medley Senior Scholarship, and marriage to Mary could have become a reality but Mr Wilson Snr was experiencing a second period of unemployment, so instead of a wedding, Harold paid his parents' rent. Harold became an assistant to William Beveridge whose report provided the basis for the postwar Welfare State and, in particular, the National Health Service.

The happy wedding ceremony eventually took place on the very first day of 1940. By then, Harold had already volunteered for active service following the outbreak of war. But the country was in greater need of his brilliant brains than his willing brawn. So he was classed as a specialist and seconded into the Civil Service in a reserved occupation. He proved to be an invaluable statistician and economist for the essential coal industry. By 1943, he was Director of Economics and Statistics for Fuel and Power.

As soon as the war ended, Harold decided to go into politics, becoming MP for Ormskirk, a market town between Liverpool and Southport. He also wrote his first book, *A New Deal For Coal*, proposing that nationalisation would increase efficiency and productivity. On taking up his seat in the House, he was immediately appointed Parliamentary Secretary to the Ministry of Works. Two years later, as Secretary for Overseas Trade, he negotiated with the Soviet Union for exports to

Britain. In some quarters these official visits to Moscow were misinterpreted and his loyalties were called into question.

By 1947, Wilson had become President of the Board of Trade and in 1950, the newly created seat of Huyton, Liverpool, became his constituency. With his warm, Northern accent, his pipe, dog and Gannex mac as his trademarks, Wilson became a 'man of the people'. He was noted for his witty speeches, always clearly expressed and easy to follow. Thanks to his powers of persuasion, by the time he was Shadow Chancellor on the Opposition benches, he was able to defeat the then government's Finance Bill.

He had a knack of inventing phrases that stayed in the public's memory. 'The Gnomes of Zurich', alluding to Swiss financiers, was one of his. So was 'the pound in your pocket', 'a week is a long time in politics', and 'thirteen years of Tory mis-rule'. When asked his opinion on the Profumo Affair that rocked the Conservative and Liberal parties, his answer was 'No comment . . . in glorious Technicolour!'

Harold enjoyed the theatre, offered to prompt for the D'Oyly Carte's Gilbert and Sullivan operettas, made sure The Beatles were awarded the MBE, created

Mary Wilson, Harold Wilson, Ken Dodd and Bessie Braddock.

knighthoods for show business moguls and made the Forces' Sweetheart, Vera Lynn, a dame. He also realised it was time to abolish censorship in the theatre. The era of the mini-skirt, flower-power and hippy hairstyles was just around the corner.

In the 1964 election, Labour won by a narrow majority. Wilson became Prime Minister but within eighteen months it became necessary to protect this weak situation with a further election. By this time the country had warmed to Wilson and Labour gained a comfortable majority of ninety-six seats. In 1966, the war in Vietnam brought problems for Wilson. He 'dissociated' the British Government from President Johnson's bombing of Hanoi and would not let Britain be drawn into the situation. It was also in 1966 that Wilson withdrew British military forces from east of Suez, thus hastening the closing days of the British Empire. Wilson clashed with Tom Smith regarding the situation in Rhodesia, claiming that Smith constantly 'moved the goalposts' over the question of independence. Devaluation of the pound in 1967 was an unpopular move but it did bring about some improvement in the country's floundering economy.

Despite his conventional background, Wilson was very much a forward-thinking man. Many aspects taken for granted in present-day life are due to Wilson's influence. He realised that some laws were becoming archaic and untenable. As well as the end of censorship, his term of office saw the abolition of capital punishment, changes in the law concerning abortion and the liberalisation of attitudes towards homosexual relationships between consenting adults in private. Remembering with gratitude that, for him, reaching the heights of academia would have been impossible without generous grants and scholarships, he made more grants available for talented working-class youngsters. The idea of comprehensive schooling was introduced by his governments. More universities were created, thus opening up opportunities for a greater influx of female students. Wilson's first constituency of Ormskirk is now home to Edge Hill University College. The creation of the Open University is probably one of the most popular innovations for which he is remembered, especially by housewives already bringing up a family.

1970 saw an unexpected defeat for Labour, but Wilson remained as Leader of the Labour Party and was returned for a second term as Prime Minister in 1974. A clever move on his part was to call for a referendum on Britain's entry into the Common Market. This unique event settled the question with the minimum of disruption. Trouble was brewing nearer to home, however. Strife was fermenting in Northern Ireland and the situation would flare up time and time again over the years to come.

As time went by, Wilson began to detect worrying changes within himself. His phenomenal memory began to deteriorate and he realised that the former young prodigy was ageing more rapidly than his contemporaries. He began to entertain paranoid ideas. He thought his rooms were bugged and that secret agents, possibly South African or Russian, were plotting against him. Even when he and Mary were holidaying on their beloved Scilly Isles, Wilson was still troubled. Seeing fishing trawlers, he feared they might be Russian spy ships in disguise.

Wilson's private life was troubled. There was much resentment against Wilson's personal assistant, Marcia Williams. She was considered by many to be the 'power behind the throne'. Unsubstantiated hints and suggestions of an improper relationship seeped under the doors that led to the corridors of power. While these rumours never troubled Mary Wilson, who wrote poetry and stayed well clear of politics, Harold was irritated and unsettled to the point of suing one pop group who made some insinuations in their lyrics. Although Mary and Marcia remained the best of friends, even after Marcia became Baroness Falkender and even after Harold's death, this did nothing to silence the gossip.

Although he had previously mentioned it to the queen, Wilson's sudden and unexpected announcement of his resignation while still in office shocked many of his colleagues. Historically, previous prime ministers had been at the height of their powers at his age. Marcia Falkender remained unpopular with important figures such as Haines, Tony Benn and the Oxford sage, Lord Goodman. Many questioned her influence over such matters as Wilson's resignation honours list. This had been passed on in her own handwriting on her famous lavender coloured notepaper. She claimed that she had merely made a neat copy of someone else's almost illegible scribble.

Following his resignation, in spite of gradually failing mental powers, Wilson did all he could to make things smooth and straightforward for his successor, James Callaghan.

Harold and Mary then lived in quiet retirement until his death in 1995. The controversies surrounding Wilson's latter years in power continued for many years and are, to a certain extent, still unresolved to this day.

Stephen Yip

Founder of the Charity KIND –
Kids in Need and Distress

Throughout the ages, there have always been some enlightened individuals who have looked around their home surroundings and said to themselves, 'Something is wrong here. And I'm the one to put it right.' Stephen Yip is one of that visionary band.

In the heart of inner-city Liverpool, there is a secret garden, about the size of a postage stamp, where disadvantaged children can find hope, encouragement and self-confidence. It is hidden away behind Canning Street, in the shadow of the Anglican Cathedral's imposing tower. Back Canning Street is hardly more than an alleyway, originally intended as the tradesmen's entrance for the large terraced houses of the Victorian era. But the lower end of this cobbled passageway connects with Hope Street, such an appropriate name for the home of the charity known as KIND.

Stephen Yip and his siblings were born and brought up in the famous back-to-back houses of Duke Terrace, Liverpool 1. These diminutive dwellings, with no gardens, no back yard and no back entrance, originally only had three rooms and a basement. In years gone by, a separate family would have occupied the basement. By 1950 when the Yip family lived there, the accommodation had been enlarged simply by making two back-to-back houses into one home. The adjoining back walls were opened up, thus doubling the number of rooms and giving each home two separate points of access via a 'front' door at both back and front. As the Yip family numbered ten in total, eight children and two parents, this was more of a necessity than a bonus. There had also been two other babies but sadly both had died.

Mr Loy Yip was a long-distance seaman, sometimes away from home for months at a time, so the youngsters grew up in a predominantly matriarchal environment. Fortunately, Mrs Betty Yip was an excellent mother, capable and loving, with a natural, warm-hearted sense of discipline. From their father they learned the excellent Chinese tradition of respect for one's elders. At an early age, the children understood right from wrong and they learned to share and care for others. As they lived next door to a police station, they often played near the black marias and the police horses. One day, when some of them were caught pinching sweets from a nearby shop, their mother marched them into the 'Nick' and made sure they received a severe dressing-down. Then she made them pay for the sweets and offer an apology. Times were not easy. Basic foods and very few toys were the order of the day. Leisure time was spent playing in the inner-city streets or wandering around the dock area. The children never had a holiday until the eldest siblings started work. Stephen says, 'My own children can't understand that Christmas presents consisted of a small stocking filled with fruit, nuts and a book. As a child it

Stephen prepares the SEED garden at the KIND centre.

took me a long time to realise why all the books were already written in, saying "with love to" and then some stranger's name.'

Stephen's first school was in Pleasant Street. Then, on winning a scholarship at the age of eleven, he took a daily bus journey out to the suburbs, to Quarry Bank High School, now called Calderstones School. Here he mixed with the children of professional families and became particularly friendly with a boy called Ian Collins whose father was a Senior Inspector for the NSPCC. The boys often acted as volunteer collectors on flag days. At the age of fifteen, they began accompanying groups of deprived children to summer holiday camps. During the next few years, Stephen gained valuable experience in fund-raising and the organising of vacations for underprivileged youngsters. In 1975, when Stephen was nineteen, he discovered that no holiday had been arranged, so he decided he would do something to help. More than that, he would set up a new charity for kids in need and distress and then take full responsibility for the whole project.

His first small step for mankind consisted of providing Christmas presents for the most needy families in his own neighbourhood. Managing to obtain fifty empty hampers and persuade local firms to supply the contents, Stephen and his volunteers played Santa Claus to children who would have had nothing at all but for KIND, the name of Stephen's newly formed charity – standing for Kids in Need and Distress.

By the following summer, with just £500 in donations, he was able to give his first group of deprived youngsters a break in the country. Stephen stresses that these breaks are not just aimless holidays. 'I could see that the need was much greater than that,' he explains. 'I wanted to create an opportunity for boys and girls to realise their own full potential. To me, every child has worth. Hope for a better future must be nurtured to ensure that their development takes a positive route. We help to foster life skills, better relationships and an awareness of citizenship that

Stephen in the SEED garden with the type of mangle which would have been used by Kitty Wilkinson.

nay be lacking when they first come to us. Our little referrals arrive via health
isitors, social services, schools and community groups. We provide training in
verything from laying the table properly to pony trekking, nature study, craft
kills, drama and film-making to improve communication and confidence. Children
lso grow and gather food ingredients and learn how to cook nutritious meals.
Many of them have no idea that hens lay eggs and peas grow from seeds. We also
ncourage tolerance, sharing and genuine, lasting friendships.'

For many years, KIND was able to take children to Balbeg House, set in many
cres of the South Ayrshire countryside. Their new rural retreat is at the Redridge
Centre, Cefn Coch, Powys. Stephen's latest project is the extension to the premises
t Back Canning Street. This represents an example of the most eco-friendly design
nd building for many miles around. It includes solar power, recycled rain water
nd thermal insulation. There are teaching areas, a dining room, a teaching kitchen,
 multi-purpose conservatory and access by lift to all floors and to the roof play
rea. The garden is a beautiful little haven with a pond, a kitchen garden and
lower beds. The garden is known as the SEED Centre, as it encourages Social and
Environmental Education and Development. 'We want children to enjoy coming
nere and to absorb experiences which help them to become happier and more
esponsible citizens,' explains Stephen.

All of the new developments have been achieved by Stephen's dynamic flair for
und-raising. The genes of altruistic visionaries from previous centuries must have
ravelled through the ether to inspire Stephen's personality. Stephen is an
accomplished and engaging public speaker, who knows how to appeal to his
audience's generosity. He is also an astute businessman, having raised millions of
pounds for the welfare of his protégés. 'It sometimes crosses my mind,' he says with
 smile, 'that if I'd opened a commercial business of some sort, I'd have been a
millionaire by now!'

But then he admits that this life has brought so much more satisfaction and
ulfilment and is really all the personal wealth that he could ever wish for.

Acknowledgements

There are three people whose life's works have benefited me enormously in the production of this book, despite the fact that they could never have known of my existence. I am indebted to the brilliance of Mr Charles Babbage (1779–1869), Dr Peter Mark Roget (1791–1871) and to Mr Oxford Concise!

And now for the present-day people. Without the computer savvy, the supreme patience and the truly friendly assistance of Eileen Brewer, I could never have completed this book in the five months between commission and finalisation. Her skills and personal interest mean so much to me.

I have also been amazingly fortunate in my two stalwarts, Dougie Redman and Peter Ware. Both have helped me enormously with the photographs and scanning of images. Again their patience has been remarkable.

For reproductions of archive material I am most grateful to Tony Hall at the *Liverpool Post And Echo*, Roger Hull at Liverpool Central Library, Johanna Booth at the Walker Art Gallery, everyone at *City* magazine, everyone at the Nugent Care Home, Maire Pierce Moulton and Sue Curbishley at the Liverpool Medical Institution, the manager and staff at the Dr Duncan Pub owned by Cain's Brewery and the manager and staff at the Fur And Feather Social Club.

I cannot speak highly enough of Jan Thomas of Ronald McDonald House at Alder Hey Children's Hospital and Madeleine Fletcher at the Imagine Charity Appeal, also at Alder Hey, for their unstinting help and kind introduction to further interesting and selfless people.

Practical help and encouragement from Geoff Woodcock PhD, Dr Bill and Mrs Nan McKean, Mrs Ronnie Finn and from Dr Tony Gilbertson have been greatly appreciated. The understanding and support of my personal friends is always of immense importance to me, especially recently while I have been writing this book and Michelle Tilling of the History Press has been a tower of strength, calm, confident and always most pleasant and helpful.

Last but most importantly, my gratitude to all the present-day celebrities and their agents, without whose willing co-operation, phone calls, letters, emails and photographs, this book could not have been written. I thank them all and hope they are pleased to be included.